CW00819058

WHAT ARE GHOSTS

AND

HOW TO EXORCISE THEM

BY

MIKE WILLIAMSON

WHAT ARE GHOSTS

AND

HOW TO EXORCISE THEM

Text by Mike Williamson unless otherwise stated.

ISBN 9780993021824

British Library Cataloguing in Publication Data.

A catalogue record for this book is available

From the British Library

Published 2016 by Mike Williamson

www.mikewilliamson.org.uk

CONTENTS

BOOK TWO

BOOK ONE

Prologue

This book is a partial history of religion and its beliefs and how they impact on our thinking about the supernatural. I have tried to show how the views of early man have had such a significant influence on the thoughts of people today, about the belief in the Devil and demons, poltergeists, ghosts, evil spirits, etc. That they are all myths that have been propagated by religions across the world to encourage people to worship their god. How there was a momentous change in religious thinking when humankind moved from many gods (Polytheism) to one God (Monotheism). How hauntings are nothing more than negative or lost spirits trying to interact with this world for either help or to cause fear and discomfort. Spirits are just people who have died; they can be negative or positive depending on their circumstances and awareness, yet most spirits move on from this world without causing any problems.

Even today there is a belief in lucky charms and superstition that runs through our everyday thoughts. The examples of possession and hauntings that we hear about more and more are nothing more than the spirits of people who have died playing on our beliefs. For example, if you believe the Devil is attacking you then that's what the spirits will show you. They will prey on your fears to get the greatest effect. The more you believe demons can attack you, the Devil, ghosts and the like, the more vulnerable you are to interference.

How the more advanced medical science has become, the fewer people believe the disease is the work of evil spirits, yet even today there are places around the world where exorcisms are performed to cure people of disease. How religious rituals still play a big part in supposedly removing unwanted spirits regardless of whether they are evil or lost and where they think they end up.

I have examined how and why spirits get lost and show examples of how to help them find peace. How some may not even know that they are causing discomfort and pain to the living. I have discussed the different beliefs of some of the major religions regarding life after death and how they consider people will attain eternal peace.

Preface

There has been a lot of media coverage about hauntings and ghostly activities, and much of it is sensationalism. Heads spinning round, and bodies floating above the ground are just filmmakers' dramatics to enhance a story. In my experience, these things don't happen. I have been visiting haunted houses for 35 years, and although I've come across things happening that are frightening, they almost always affect the emotions and feelings. Occasionally, I have found people who are experiencing physical attacks and once examined, most have been explained by little-known illnesses. An example is the following:

I visited a man who was, in his words "getting his hair pulled out during the night", and in the morning his pillow was covered in hair. He was also waking up to find half his eyebrows were missing. During the day, he felt as though someone was plucking his hair and eyebrows and sticking pins in his face. He thought he was getting attacked by spirits. It turned out his hair loss was due to too strong a dose of a particular medication. He went to his doctor who lowered the dose, and after a few weeks, his hair started growing back, leaving no hair on his pillows.

He kept two large tanks of tropical fish in his lounge where he spent most of his day. He had just got the second tank and started feeling as though his eyebrows were being plucked out as well as a rash appearing on his face. He was convinced he was being attacked by a spirit as it only happened at home. He went into the hospital for a few days, and while there he experienced no plucked eyebrows and no rash. When he returned home, it started again. We noticed the water pumps were on all the time, and the atmosphere was damp, due to the continual splashing of water in the tanks. As the water wasn't clean, the air was contaminated with tiny spores from the fish tanks. That caused his skin to react with a rash and discomfort from what appeared to be pin pricks. We suggested he spend as little time as possible in the lounge for a week, which he did, and his skin cleared up, the rash went, and he no longer suffered pin pricks. He removed one of the tanks and has had no trouble since.

This goes to show that we must look to the earthly first and, if no rational cause can be found, then possibly it may be a spirit.

Another gentleman I went to see was complaining of scratches appearing from nowhere on his back.

He thought he was under spiritual attack as it happened some nights then it would be a week before it happened again. The scratches were where he couldn't reach. I asked if he had seen a doctor, however, he said he couldn't tell the doctor that a spirit was attacking him. We went along to his house, and after checking the house out we reassured him that no spirits were attacking him, but he and his wife were terrified nonetheless. We asked him to go to the doctor and request a referral to a dermatologist, as we thought it was a skin complaint. A week later he telephoned to say the doctor thought it was Chronic Idiopathic Urticarial (Hives).

That put his mind at rest, and about a month later it was confirmed, and the medication is working as he has had no more scratches. But the dermatologist said it could flare up at any time.

So, as you can see, it's better to get physical problems checked by the doctor first before blaming ghosts or spirits.

It's easy to blame spirit for things, especially when it seems impossible for there to be any other cause. I blame this on sensational media and films. There are a plethora of television programmes about ghost hunting, hauntings, and paranormal investigations, and although things do go bump in the night, don't believe all that you hear or see.

The Origins of Negative Spirits

Why are we afraid of noises during the night or seeing ghosts? The belief in death and the hereafter is linked directly with the rise of religion. The speculation about life after death has been with religious thoughts since the beginnings of man. It's clearly uncertain how much primitive man acknowledged the idea of an afterlife. I have tried to set out the following within a historical perspective as much as possible.

The idea of death and the hereafter may have begun like this during the times of primitive man. In explaining the history of death, the afterlife, and good and evil spirits, it must be made clear that many different religions accept this notion.

Primitive ideas began with the concept of animism. This idea is mainly defined as the belief that things in nature, e.g. trees, the sky, and mountains, have souls or consciousness and the belief that people have spirits that do or can exist separately from our bodies. The creation of the supernatural was brought up by the man himself, as opposed to an almighty being that created the existence of life as we know it. We can see the analogy that the idea of entering another life, came about from the thoughts and desires of man himself.

The concept of good and evil spirits controlling the hereafter set the roots for what later became the major religions of today. It's entirely feasible that certain images began to evolve in what ultimately became established thoughts about an afterlife. There is an acceptance that it's light and peaceful in heaven and only good people are allowed in, whereas it's dark and fearful in hell, and only the evil are taken there. We need to see why such a theory was invented in the first place.

It would seem the idea of good and evil realms in the afterlife were formed to bring harmony to man's physical life; another idea is it was to bring hope to primitive man as he may have been afraid of death.

Religions with Multiple Gods

Most researchers who have studied the topic accept that religion is an important part of all human societies. No communities have survived long without it, but we can't assume that all faiths believe in the hereafter, specifically the afterlife of the soul. It's probable that worries about the afterlife are a relatively new concern in the history of human evolution. We'll go back to about 1.4 million years ago, when our ancestors migrated from the forests of Africa to the African plains. The only way to survive at that time was hunting animals and gathering food from natural resources. They barely managed to survive having reduced to perhaps as few as 5000 individuals at some point in our early history. They were not good hunters as they didn't have the size, or agility, and inborn specialised abilities of the prey they sought or of the predators that sought them. Their tendency to gather in tribes was essential to their survival as safety in numbers was critical in those perilous times. It was dangerous to wander off on your own because there were predators everywhere.

It's said these early tribes were egalitarian, meaning people who supported a social system in which everyone has equal status and the same opportunities. In the initial stages of human civilisation, sharing the responsibilities for the welfare of the tribe appears to have been the key to survival. Individuals who attempted to impose their will on the group were likely to be banished or executed. Early tribes were made up of relatively small bands of people, and internal tribal unity was necessary for cooperative hunting, food sharing and success in intertribal warfare. They were protective of their territory as food wasn't that abundant, and they would fight other tribes to keep their food stocks. The more closely connected and loyal the members were to each other the more likely they were to survive, this included the willingness to fight and maybe die for the tribe.

It appears that for this sort of bonding to take place rituals play an important part in common activities. Not many of nature's secrets had been discovered, so "natural" causes for the surplus or shortage of food, rain or drought, birth, and death were mysteries. The human brain is created to look for explanations for why things do or don't happen, and if answers are not obvious, we make them up. Explanations that would carry an understanding with them, which would satisfy primitive man's uneducated minds, concerning the activities of the supernatural. Such as gods, the sun, and the moon, spirits and ghosts, etc. and other forces seen and unseen, believed to be in control of practical issues. When these agents were known, ways of persuading them were created. These tactics would include dancing, singing, blood-letting, sacrifices and other ritualistic practices, designed to bring good luck to the tribe and to avoid it from being the recipient of supernatural anger.

A common feature of hunting and gathering tribes was ancestor worship. Tribespeople, who had died, continued to exist in the minds of surviving relatives and sometimes appeared in dreams during the night. When not visiting the minds of the living, ancestors were thought to exist as spirits dwelling in the sky, under the ground, in trees, high grasses, on mountain tops, and in the bodies of various animals, or surviving in completely different states. In a lot of ways ancestors who had died were perfect candidates to be acknowledged as being able to perform both good and evil deeds. A fundamental part of ancestor worship was, and still is in some areas of the world, that the ancestors remain part of this world. No matter what form their spirits take, the dead were thought to continue to take an interest and be quite influential in tribal affairs. It was believed that by giving them proper burials, gifts, and sacrifices, spirits of the deceased could be persuaded to cure illnesses, increase or decrease the food supply, and give the tribe resourcefulness and courage to overthrow their enemies. In some societies, they would be called upon for advice, on how to deal with people who disrupted the customs of egalitarianism, or who were not sharing the burdens of the tribe. The existing social order was preserved in this and other ways, by consulting with their ancestors.

To honour and celebrate their ancestors and the supernatural, tribespeople would engage in ritualised singing and group dancing (occasionally until they were in a delirious and trance-like state), which were important occasions for group bonding. These rituals provided members with a strong sense of group involvement, and with that involvement, a sense of group safety and continuity.

We don't know if the hunters and gatherers believed in a personal soul that continues in the hereafter. It's unlikely that they believed in a soul until missionaries tried to introduce the idea centuries later. It isn't known if tribesmen looked forward to dying in the hope of being held in higher regard by the tribe. The living had bodies, and the dead people became spirits, and the primary goal of both the deceased and the living was the unity and close relationship with the tribe.

There are still some hunter and gathering tribes surviving today. The Hadza in northern Tanzania and The Pirahas in Brazil. Both of whom have been studied intensively and have been found to be minimalists as far as afterlife beliefs are concerned. The Hadza consider death as a matter of course. They are born to live for as long they live; they die, and that's it. Burial rights are modest, and a belief in an afterlife doesn't appear to exist. During these studies, it was found their present-day activities consisted of finding and or catching food and eating it immediately instead of conserving some for future use.

The Pirahas represent another illustration of a hunter and gathering tribe that lives in the present and gives minimum or no thought about life tomorrow, never mind life in the hereafter. The Pirahas are made up of small Indian tribes living on the banks of the Amazon River in Brazil.

The Pirahas are exceptionally democratic; there are no elected leaders or chiefs in the tribe. All members treat all other tribespeople as equal, everything of value like canoes, bows and arrows and food are shared. Nobody is richer or poorer, and there is no interest in collecting material wealth. Immediate experience is all that matters, and it is regarded as the knowledge of the tribe. No attention is given to the future; it's of no concern. For instance, hardly any attention is paid to preserving food; when fish is caught, they gather round and eat, no matter what time of day. History is of no interest, and no interest is paid to hearsay assertions; only eyewitness reports are accepted as facts. If a member of the tribe dies, the only reasonable reason for the death is the person was not robust enough to survive.

Being better than anyone else or improving one's conditions is of no concern, as the Pirahas emphasis is on living in the present. Plus, knowing how to deal with whatever their harsh environment has to offer is how they have survived for indefinite centuries. They are happy and surprisingly content in the context of their difficult conditions of life. Warfare is unknown to them; they are guided by moral values of fairness and sharing and to be created by God is unknown to them. They listen to the spirits of whom they are aware and see every day. As indicated earlier, the function of these spirits is to offer guidance for preserving social order.

We are unsure whether the Pirahas of Brazil and the Hadza tribe in Tanzania are today's examples of ancient hunting and gathering tribes. But they may give us an idea about afterlife beliefs before the development of farming communities. From the above, hunting and gathering tribes didn't believe people had souls that leave the body at the point of death or were rewarded or punished depending on how the lived their lives. It's unlikely that tribes so entirely focused on life in the present and who were not inclined to plan for the future, would be able to imagine themselves living forever in better or poorer conditions. Dead or alive, their undisputed purpose was to preserve well-practiced traditions keeping the tribe together for the sake of individual and group survival.

As the hunting and gathering tribes had no perception of an afterlife, they would have no reason to fear devils and demons. All who had passed before them in their memory would be loved ones and tribe members, who would be looking after the welfare of the tribe. It was their ancestors they believed who, depending on the tributes, would grant good crops, etc. or not. There were no mythical beings just loved ones and tribe members.

Creation of Farming Communities

About 13,000 years BCE, daily living began to change considerably when farming communities began to develop. Small groups of farmers and herders came together and became large settlements, and gradually egalitarianism was replaced by hierarchical, top-down governing structures. As mentioned earlier, in the ritualised hunting and gathering tribal dances, participants would enter trance -like states, with the help of plants that induced hallucinations that put them in direct contact with the spirits. This kind of group activity helped with group bonding. But bonding within small groups in large communities dedicated to growing crops, looking after livestock and trading goods with other settlements, became less functional. Different means to maintain social order had to be found. When governing large communities, it was common to adopt a layered social structure. Priesthoods emerged as rules became more diversified resulting in only members of the priesthood being entitled to communicate with the gods. The ruling elite and the spiritual leaders were in close communication all of the time, and the idea that the state and the church could or should be separate was unthinkable.

The change in time perspective was instrumental in the change from egalitarianism to a more apportioned social structure. While the hunting and gathering, tribes were living in the here and now, it was essential for farming communities to become more oriented on the future. The obvious reason was that farming required planning. You had to plant crops at the right time of the year, and previous experience guided what was likely to happen in the future. Looking after animals is also a seasonal activity, so they had to consider where the best pastures were and at what time of the year was most appropriate, to get the best from them for the herds. They also had to decide when to store animal feed for winter feeding and preserve food for human consumption, and this required complex consideration.

When a man thinks of the future, it usually requires the thinker to project an image of themselves and observe the actions they might take in an imagined scenario. Certainly, hunters and gatherers engaged in mental time travel, as they would have used their experience to predict when animals were likely to migrate. It's not likely they were able to think in the future "what if" thinking, that farmers in later communities did. They had to, to preserve food and produce for the future, and stockpile the excess for trade. The point is the more one participates in thinking about the future, especially the sort of thinking that requires projecting images of oneself into the future, the more likely one is to wonder about what happens to that projected image of the self after the death.

It's possible that hunters and gatherers could have been worried about death, and perhaps it was always on their mind. But it's more likely such fears became amplified in larger forward focused societies. Some explanations about the problem of death were used as powerful instruments for social management. For instance, if you do good deeds in this life, then you will be rewarded in eternity. Or, you will receive an eternity of punishment if you disregard the laws and do evil deeds. Naturally, the directives were decided by the chiefs and cooperating priests. It wouldn't be easy to imagine a more efficient way of bringing about social control.

People focused on communicating directly with the supernatural in the ancestral religions, through dreams and trances, requesting practical help such as good hunting, children or good health. However, in the modern religions, priests focused people's attention toward the hereafter, with the instructions to live their present lives doing deeds that would reward them in eternity.

The critical issue of what constitutes the soul is causing a lot of dispute between religions, and what happens to it when it leaves the body. For instance, the actions and rituals that are necessary in this life to assure safe passage to eternal life, and whether the soul will be rewarded or punished in the next life.

Irrespective of all the discussions and uncertainty, one thing remains clear, matters related to the continuation of life after death have occupied the thoughts of our ancestors at least since the rise of agricultural societies. Exactly how many thousands of years ago, is unclear because of the absence of written records.

One of the earliest accounts of the emergence of concern for the next life is the story of Gilgamesh. Gilgamesh was a Babylonian King, who ruled around 2700 BCE. By 2000 BCE he had become a hero. His story was written on tablets in the Sumerian language and were widely dispersed in Mesopotamia, so we know that the search for immortality has been of keen interest for at least 4000 years. The legend of Gilgamesh is not the source of the great religious myths of our time because the solution to the problem of life after death that he discovered (there is no life after death) was not the kind of solution people wanted to hear. There was a more hopeful view of the expectations of an afterlife that was fairly well established in Ancient Egypt at about the same time that Gilgamesh was King, but the journey from death to eternal life is not inevitable.

We can see from the above how control through religion started to come about, with the priests dictating and controlling the communication with the spirits or gods. They could say what they liked, and as no one else was supposed to have access to the gods, there could be no argument.

Ancient Egypt

In Ancient Egypt, they thought that people were made up of three essential parts: the physical body, which is unique to everyone is the first part; Ba is the second part, and Ka is the third. Although the body changes as a person gets older, death is the last change. Ba is the second part that is the personality or character, an amalgamation of all non-physical things, which makes each of us different from everyone else. Ba would be made up of the thoughts and memories, preferences, the way in which you express your emotions, everything you know, your intelligence, etc. Ka is the third part that is the life force; this is the universal energy, something that is shared by all living people and does not represent the person. In the beginning, the creator made Ka and whether you have or haven't got Ka is the difference between being alive or dead.

Ba and Ka both leave the body through the mouth when it dies and go to the Underworld separately. Although the separation is not permanent (unless things don't go well), eventually Ba and Ka are reunited with the body and resurrected in the Underworld as AKH. Those who make the transition successfully, proceed to eternal life with the gods in the Underworld. Where life continues, in the same way, life is conducted above ground. Except there is no suffering, no disease, no poverty and specifically no death. In this section of the Underworld, it is a permanent, eternal, endless life. Those who fail to make the transition suffer the fate of becoming "re-dead" with no hope of resurrection. The requirements to ensure a place in the Underworld of the gods is good behaviour in this world before death. There are a few examples we will come across that demonstrate how religions work on behalf of maintaining the social order.

A lot of work had to be done by the living in preparing the body for the transition. To start with, all the organs except the heart had to be removed before the body was mummified. After this was done a comprehensive series of rituals, invocations and ceremonial offerings of food and other items were made to ensure safe passage. The deceased were given maps of the Underworld with guidelines about how to overcome obstacles they might encounter as the judgment day came closer.

Although ideas may vary, the basic form that judgment day takes is Ba is summoned to the Hall of Truth, where several gods are gathered. Osiris, the god of the Underworld, would be among them. The deceased's heart is put on one end of a scale and a feather placed on the other. With various gods, present, Ba, who represents the essence of the former person, is required to recite the following lines (only three are listed here):

"I have not done falsehood against man."

"I have done no evil."

"I have not impoverished my associates."

If the affirmation by Ba is truthful, then the scale will stay balanced perfectly. This is required before the gods will allow Ba to direct Ka to the body they formerly occupied, and thereby enter the state of AKH. But if untruths are told, the heart becomes heavy, and the scales become imbalanced, then the person is denied the resurrection.

The beliefs in Ancient Egypt are that Ba was the Egyptian equivalent of the personal soul, but never thought of as independent of the body, and was incapable of surviving by itself. It was the early Greeks who several centuries later came to the radical conclusion that the soul and the body were separate.

Now we start to see how the belief in the repercussions of not being law abiding and good could affect the life in the hereafter. Initially, it was mere thought of what would happen, but now there is a test to see if one is worthy of eternal life. Also, we find we are made up of something more than a physical body, and there is a definite place we will go depending on our conduct in this life.

Ancient Greece

There are still remnants of Ancient Egyptian beliefs like the final judgment of the soul in some present-day religions. The Western world accepted the ancient Greek thoughts more than the teachings of the ancient Egyptians. I will get to the point by focusing on a few principle individuals in this long and complicated story.

Let's start with the Greek Poet Homer, author of *The Lliad* and *The Odyssey* in the 8th century BCE. There seem to be some afterlife beliefs that are common to that time in Greek history which we can extract from these heroic stories. The Greek word associated with the soul is psyche, a word linked with the word psychein, meaning to blow or breathe. Psyche is the breath of life, which is inhaled into the body at birth and exhaled out at death. But it should not be related to Ba or Ka that depart from the mouth and have the opportunity of resurrection in Egyptian Mythology. In Homers times, the Greek psyche goes straight to Hades where it exists as a shade or shadow. Hades is a dismal, dreary, miserable place where there is no hope of anything better. It was thought that shadows have no character; they don't speak, are very foolish, and they no longer exist when they are forgotten by the living. This is where every person goes, whether they are wicked of kind hearted, Hades is where all psyches become shades, and that's all there is.

When Hesiod wrote the *Isles of Blest* in the 7th century BCE, in his work titled "Works of Days", things started to get better. For the fortunate few there was an afterlife, and it was lived on the Isles of Blest as it was on the Greek mainland but without some important drawbacks. The fertile fields supplied abundant crops that they could harvest three times a year. What was even more attractive than good crops was that there was no suffering, no sorrow, and no death, on the Isles of Blest. But it was only the heroes who got killed in combat in the wars of Thebes and Troy who could reside in this paradise. As Hesiod imagined it, the good life was only available to the heroes that died in combat in the wars of Thebes and Troy. These heroes of the wars were given immortality by being transported body and soul straight to the Isles of Blest, instead of dying on the battlefields and becoming shadows in Hades.

There wasn't much specific talk about the soul by Greek poets until Plato dealt with the topic in the 5th century BCE. Pythagoras instigated the idea about a hundred years previously by beginning the process of loosening the soul from the body. Using mathematics, he made a distinction between physical objects and material things that included the body in this world and things that were non-physical. All material things have mathematical properties and abide by certain laws, one of which is that no material object can move by itself. For instance, a stone cannot move. If you want it to move, you as an external force must do the work. Another law governing the material world is two objects can't occupy the same physical space at the same time. But neither of the above rules applied to the psyches; psyches are self-moving. If you want to look in a different direction, then do it; your soul will help. The psyche does not require external assistance to move.

Considered from a certain perspective, more than one psyche can be present in the same place concurrently. For example, it could be that two minds occupy the same space temporarily when reading someone's mind. Whatever the case might be, it was evident to Pythagoras that the material world and the non-material world of the psyche could not be governed by the same laws.

We don't know what Pythagoras thought, but a good deal has been credited to him. It's also accepted that Orphic and Dionysian's resurrection myths in the 5th century BCE influenced his thinking. He was also entranced by the idea that shamans could disengage and re-engage their psyches from their bodies when they came back from extraordinary journeys. The idea that psyches could "transmigrate" from one body to another (including the bodies of animals) is also credited to Pythagoras. Whatever the actual case may have been, and depending on one's perspective, we have either been cursed or gained from his vivid suppositions.

The religious implications of Plato's observations are far-reaching and are as follows:

– The soul is of divine creation.

– The soul is immortal.

– The body and soul are two entirely separate entities.

– All souls pre-existed in other bodies.

– The soul is perfect, but that perfection is contaminated by having to be encased in the body.

It was Plato more than any other historical figure before his time, who introduced the world to full-fledged, mind-body dualism. Two entities, body and soul; bodies come and go, but souls are immortal. Souls inhabit bodies and move into other bodies when that present one dies. Plato also suggests the connection between the soul and the body it inhabits is frequently stressed. The soul doesn't like occupying the body partly because it is contaminated by the body and partly because it would prefer to be free. Plato modified this one against one struggle 20 years later in his book *The Republic*, in which he divided the soul into two elements: a rational part (governed by higher reason) and an irrational element (governed by lower basic appetites). He also suggested a third component: the will or spirit. The spirit can either side with reason or irrational desires giving the person a choice. There is one way a soul can stop the cycle of reincarnation, and that is to operate in the rational sphere of reason because beauty and truth can only be gained by pure reason. But pure reason is hard to maintain because it's under threat of being overwhelmed by the basic appetites of the body like pleasure, lust, pain, envy, fear, and hope. Plato suggests that when the soul reaches perfection, it no longer needs to reincarnate thus ending the cycle of rebirth.

Plato emphasised the struggle between the material body and the ethereal soul. The body could not operate without the soul, and it was nearly impossible for the soul not to be contaminated by the body. The tension between maintaining purity of the soul subsequently became the central feature of Christian and Islamic religion as we will see.

Now the body has a symbiotic relationship with the soul (meaning living together in the same body), made up of a soul that is a separate entity from the body. We also see that the soul is immortal and exists by travelling from one body to another. There is also a suggestion that the soul can end the continuous reincarnations by becoming pure, but it will take many incarnations to achieve.

Considering Plato's ideas about multiple incarnations of the soul leads me to suggest some features of the Hindu religion which promote beliefs that are compatible with Plato's idea that souls released from dead bodies are reincarnated into new bodies. The repeated reincarnations only end after the soul reaches perfection. This idea predated Plato by several centuries in the northern regions of India and is one of the many instances of the dispersion of ideas over long distances and long periods of time.

HINDUISM

Extract from Wikipedia

The overriding feature of Hinduism is the reincarnation of the soul with the ultimate goal of ending the cycle of rebirth.

Hinduism isn't a single religion like Zoroastrianism, Judaism, Islam, and Christianity, it's a mixture or combination of three religious traditions. There's no sole founder or precise time of origin. It's a long-term accumulation of some religious views into a commonly accepted system of salvation. The ultimate goal of Hinduism is to find release from the cycle of rebirths and acquire unity with the Ultimate Reality. This oneness results in the final release of the soul from the continuous recycling into various physical forms. You'll notice no single god has been mentioned, only something called the Ultimate Reality, and salvation is a process that involves repeated re-births. Where the "Western" monotheistic perspective proposes one God, one path to salvation and only one lifetime to get there, Hinduism suggests many lives and three alternate routes to becoming at one with the Ultimate Reality. The three paths are the Path of Devotion, The Upanisadic Goal of Release from Rebirth (also known as Path of Knowledge) and Path Ritual

Salvation. Because people are in different stages of their progression toward salvation, everyone is free to select the path most suited to their religious needs.

Zoroastrianism

Zoroastrianism was founded approximately 3500 years ago, by the prophet Zoroaster in ancient Iran. It's one of the oldest monotheistic religions in the world. It was the official religion of Persia – now known as Iran – from 650BCE to 600 BCE, and one of the most powerful.

Zoroastrians have only one God called Ahura Mazda (Wise Lord), who created the world.

Zoroaster was born into a Bronze Age culture with a polytheistic religion (worship of many gods) that included animal sacrifice and the ritual use of intoxicants, like early Hinduism. He rejected the Bronze Age religion with their many gods and oppressive class structure in which princes and priests controlled the ordinary people. When he was 30 years old, he had a divine vision of Ahura Mazda (God) and five other radiant beings, Amesha Spentas (Holy Immortals). He had many subsequent visions during which he asked many questions, the answers forming the foundations of Zoroastrian religion. Ahura Mazda had his counterpart in the name of Angra Mainyu (Destructive Spirit), the originator of death and all the evil in the world.

Ahura Mazda, who is perfect, resides in heaven, whereas Angra Mainyu lives in the depths of Hell. When someone dies, they will go to the appropriate place depending on their deeds during their lifetime.

Dualism in Zoroastrianism is the existence of, although complete separation of good and evil, which is recognised in two ways: Cosmically (opposing forces within the universe), and Morally (opposing forces within the mind).

Cosmic dualism refers to the ongoing fight between good (Ahura Mazda) and evil (Angra Mainyu) within the universe.

Angra Mazda is the destructive energy that opposes God's creative energy, and not God's equal opposite. This creative power is called Spenta Mainyu; God used his creative energy to manifest a perfect world that Angra Mainyu continually attacks, making it impure. Sickness, famine, aging, natural disasters, death and so on are accredited to Angra Mainyu. With universal dualism, we have life and death, day and night, good and evil; one cannot be without the other and life is a mixture of two opposing forces.

Moral dualism refers to the opposition of good and evil in the mind of humankind, truth, and deception, etc. emphasising that we have a choice. This choice is essential as it determines whether we are a helper of Ahura Mazda or Angra Mainyu. When all of humankind chooses the former over the latter, evil will finally be defeated, and paradise on earth will be realised. Zoroastrianism has a positive outlook, and it teaches that humankind is ultimately good and that this goodness will finally triumph over evil.

It's accepted that in Abrahamic religions, the concepts of heaven and hell, as well as the Devil, were heavily influenced by Zoroastrian belief.

Here we have a religion that existed alongside Ancient Egypt and Greece, and this is the first mention of evil as a separate and opposing force to God. It is the first time the opposing force has been given a name Angra Mainyu (Destructive Spirit), and this was 1200 years before Judaism.

Modern Zoroastrian, Judaic, Christian and Islamic religions feature one God. Since the Christian and Islamic religions were both derived from Judaism, this one God is the same for all three faiths. As Zoroastrianism, predated Judaism and the visions given to the Prophet Zoroaster and Abraham are very similar, therefore it's reasonable to assume there was some influence from Zoroastrian beliefs in the message Abraham was given. The worshipping of only one God is called monotheism, and the Zoroastrianism religion was the first to worship in this way in about 1500 BCE in ancient Iran. This was 1200 years before Judaism which appeared in the 3rd century BCE. Before 1500 BCE in the rest of the known world polytheism reigned with multiple deities being worshipped. There were rain gods and wind gods, sea gods who controlled the tides, gods and goddesses of love and happiness and deities of destruction, death and doom. There were gods of war, good times and bad times. There were household goddesses, gods of health fertility gods and separate gods that reigned over almost every aspect of nature. There were main gods, like sun gods, and smaller gods like the Egyptian deities that looked after lungs, liver, stomach and intestines (two gods per organ).

You will remember Gilgamesh was informed by the gods (not God) and in Egyptian mythology, they joined the gods in the Underground of eternal life and the gods of the hunter-gatherers.

Judaism

It took several hundred years for the concept of a single God to take hold, and it was not until the Israelite God Yahweh arrived that things started to change.

The idea of a single God didn't suddenly come on a particular date, and it took centuries for the idea to be accepted, a one and only true God. But when it did it was the beginning of a massive change in how people thought of the supernatural and became the foundation of modern day Judaic, Islamic and Christian religions.

Before the ancient Israelites raised Yahweh to his position of absolute supremacy, he was considered to be at the same level as other gods of competing nations. The Israelites relied on Yahweh to see them through tough times to authorise war, and guide them to victory, or to recommend restraint. Struggles between nations became battles between gods and a major victory implied "Our god is better than your god" and those who lost were left to wonder why their god let them down.

There were political, and economic benefits involved in the emergence of one God. One of these was that it was good to have as many trading partners as possible for the financial health and well- being of the nations involved. But that was only providing the trading nations benefitted by the arrangement. It didn't matter who worshipped who so long as the trade was going well. When things didn't go smoothly, or one nation invaded another, then the leaders of the conquering nation had a choice. They could either let the conquered people continue to worship their god(s) and acknowledge that gods other than their own existed, a condition called monolatry, or they could ban the worship of gods other than their own. Looking at the Old Testament, we can see there was religious tolerance in some cases. An angry god, a god who insists on being the only one, or a god who is intent on blood and vengeance usually won. Yahweh's rise to supreme power in the minds of the Jewish theologians didn't come about because ancient Jews were always successful in protecting their land or taking over the territory of their enemies. It might have happened because of significant defeats. The Babylonians had conquered Israelite land and belittled their god by destroying his temple in Jerusalem, and the Assyrians stripped the temple of its treasures. In other words, Yahweh rose to the top after he had suffered at the hands of Israelites enemies.

The theory is that Jewish theologians and intellectuals spent many years in exile and had plenty of time to wonder why Yahweh was so weak. Their conclusion changed the world; instead of Yahweh being one of many gods, he oversaw everything. All the gods of all the other nations were Yahweh's puppets. A new understanding of history emerged from the deliberations of these exiles when they concluded that it was Yahweh alone that had orchestrated the setbacks and defeats. Because he was angry that they continued worshipping other gods, he organised their surprising victories to show them and other nations who was the boss.

Events in the ancient nation against nation world might have given people the impression that winning or losing, depended on which deities had the most power at the time of a particular battle. That all changes when an all-knowing, all-powerful God is injected into the picture. The acceptance of this transformative idea that an unseen puppeteer had been controlling the movements of on-stage gods developed into the most enduring myth of all time. A myth that came about over many years and filled the pages of The Old Testament. This God of the Bible made all other gods irrelevant, figments of imaginations that perhaps echoed the imaginations of hunter and gathering tribes. This God, this one, and only God, is a demanding God who operates with a long-term plan. Before we look at how that plan varies in the three monotheistic religions, we must face the fact that Plato's one soul/multiple–body theory, is an inadequate basis for the type of monotheistic thoughts that began to carry the day.

The changing of national and religious loyalties was common occurrences before and during Plato's time. His statement that the soul moves from body to body until it reaches the ultimate state of truth and beauty, and that it is immortal was out of tune with the arrival of the one God viewpoint.

Aristotle (384–332 BCE), a student of Plato, disagreed with Plato's idea that the soul needs to be free from the restrictions of the body, and the soul's unpleasant relationship with the body. Aristotle emphasised the idea that the soul is what makes a body a body. As opposed to Plato's observation that the soul was a necessary encumbrance to the body, Aristotle asserted that their interdependence was an essential good. Aristotle saw the soul as providing every living organism including plants and animals with the plan of what is to become. He said souls could not exist without bodies and bodies cannot become bodies without souls. Virtually everything is ensouled to Aristotle's way of thinking. Take the chicken, it contains the potential of a chicken, but the potential cannot be realised, until the soul within orchestrates successive stages of embryonic development and creates a chicken.

Both human and non-human souls enable the organism to respond to the features of their environments that might affect their survival. Its what souls do, and they do it automatically, no thought is involved. What makes humans unique, what separates us from all other creatures, is the soul of a human contains a reflective element that enables us to think in the abstract. Aristotle used the term Nous for the highest part of the rational soul and emphasised Nous thinks in pictures, and when it is released, it is timeless, divine and immortal. Aristotle's grounding of the soul in the material body was philosophically more compatible with the one God only/one soul only view of the Old Testament, and, even more, harmonious with later Christian and Islamic beliefs that emerged in later centuries. The integration of the soul and body to create a whole person is a stronger foundation for a belief system that implies that the fate of one is interlinked with the fate of the other. If the body is identified as a temporary container for the wandering soul and is no longer relevant to any afterlife concerns once the soul has left it. If there is any hint that afterlife involves a body/soul reunion, or the fate of the soul is dependent on the part it played in the life of the body, then we best pay careful attention to the relationship between the body and the soul in real life. It was thought, we only get one life, and what is done in this life pre-determines the quality of life in the next and the next one is eternal. The best way to ensure a happy body/soul afterlife reunion is to take directions from the one God, as they have been preached by his various prophets.

The Jewish view on immortality and life after death is vague as these matters are not dealt with in the Hebrew Bible. The topic doesn't come up in the first five chapters of the Old Testament, where we're informed that in the beginning God created the earth, moulded a figure from clay, and gave the breath of life to animate it. When a person expires, they become a dead breath, and the body returns to dust and the spirit returns to God. In addition, to becoming dust the dead descend to Sheol, a place where the dead are dead. Sheol is like Homer's Hades; it is a dark, miserable place where most people are congregated together. There are exceptions where evil people's dust is excluded from resting near their family. Apart from that nothing happens, and all that's left is the intermingling of the remains of former human beings. But the idea that dead people are dead did not endure the test of time as other outcomes about life beyond the confines of Sheol were discussed. One theme has been consistent throughout the ages of Jewish thought, and that is what matters most is this life, the life currently being lived. There are plenty of Jews who care about the hereafter, but as a rule, most Jews are faithful to their traditions, which they consider more important than their fate in the hereafter. People come and go, but the Jewish tribe and its traditions are to be continued at all costs. The consequences of adhering to Jewish laws set out centuries ago have more impact on this life than on what happens in the afterlife. The people and their customs must be preserved. The idea that the soul should be stuck in Sheol forever was later varied when it was discovered in the book of Daniel, a passage that read: "And many of them that sleep in the dust of the earth shall awake, some to everlasting life, and some to reproaches and everlasting abhorrence." (Daniel 12:2)

This passage was later used to resolve the solution to a major dilemma. How did it come about that some polytheistic Jews, who disavowed Yehweh and remained true to their pagan gods, prospered while many faithful Yehwists lived in abject poverty?

Similarly upsetting was the fact that when Jews were killed in battles, both Yehwists and Jewish pagans suffered the same fate. Surviving Yehwists questioned why they should stick to a one-god-only belief system, when at the end of the day, the Yehwists' children were starving while the pagan-worshipping Jewish merchants had great feasts. The conclusion was that just rewards and just punishments would be distributed in the next life.

Ideas differed on how that would work; The School of Shammai endorsed the idea that there would be a day of judgement when righteous people would be separated from the wicked. The righteous would go to Gan Eden (Garden of Eden), and evil people would go straight to Gehinnom (Hell). Those who were in-between – who were neither purely good nor purely evil – would also be sent to Gehinnom, where they would be punished for 12 months. When fully cleansed they would be admitted to Gen Eden, but the punishment of the truly bad ones is unrelenting and only comes to an end when they are annihilated.

We must remember that The School of Shammai's view on the hereafter represents but one branch of a multi-branched religion. Most past and current rabbis point out that the hereafter is just speculation. Nobody speaks from experience. Jews don't talk much about heaven and hell; it's not that important to most Jews.

Christianity

The essential features of Christian afterlife beliefs are not in the New Testament. In fact, the New Testament contains many contradictions because the chapters were written by many people over a period of hundreds of years. Catholicism was the principal Christian religion throughout the Middle Ages with Protestantism emerging at the end of the Middle Ages, mainly due to protests against certain practices of the mother church. For instance, Martin Luther (1483–1540 CE), a leading figure in the Protestant Revolution, objected to the practice of the church being paid by Congregationalist, to lessen the time they or their loved ones spent in Purgatory, being cleansed of their sins. Regardless of the split with the Catholic Church and the explosion of alternative versions of the Christian faith, they all agree on the following principals:

Babies are born into a world of sin, as St Paul wrote, "God created humans to be pure, innocent and immortal". He did not create sin but his first creation Adam, with the assistance of Eve, did exactly that. Adam's sin polluted the world forever, and death became our common fate. So, everyone is already a sinner at birth because all are victims of Adam's original sin. The ritual of baptism is designed to cleanse the soul from the inherited sin, but baptism alone does not guarantee salvation.

Though the wages of sin are death, John the Baptist declared death could be avoided when he wrote, "For God so loved the world that he gave his only Son, that whoever believes in him should not perish but have eternal life". The only way to salvation is through Jesus Christ and if you didn't accept him into your life you were destined to go to hell. The day of judgement will come, and there are two versions of this. One in the Apocalypse according to John, Christ will return for a final battle with Satan. The battle will last for 1000 days and will end with Satan's defeat. Then all the living and dead are gathered together, and final heaven or hell judgements will be made. Regardless of the details, an essential element of Christianity is the belief in a final day of reckoning. The consequences of not being redeemed are eternal damnation. There are two deaths: one of the body that is unavoidable; the other, which can be averted by accepting Jesus and following his path to resurrection. There is still debate about the second death; whether it is to be excluded from the presence of God, or eternal damnation in the fiery pits of hell.

The consequences of salvation are everlasting life in heaven. Heaven is the destination for all people who accept Christ as their personal saviour. Most Christian churches preach that the soul reunites with the body at resurrection time. Some say the final form will be a spiritual self, but the most widely accepted model is Christ, whose body and soul were intact when he rose to heaven.

Considering the common Abrahamic origins of all three major Western religions, one should not be surprised by overlapping beliefs. Islamic and Christian afterlife beliefs are similar in many respects. The existence of heaven and hell are basic beliefs in both religions; they are both confident that a "Day of Judgement" will happen, and all will go before God and be judged depending on the lives they had lived. The virtuous will ascend to heaven, and the non-virtuous will be sent to hell.

Islam

Like Christians, Muslims believe there is no God but God.

Everything in the universe was brought into existence by God.

All things come from God and return to God.

The only people who will be resurrected will be those who believe in Him and conduct their lives according to His Words as recorded by Mohammed in the Koran.

The important difference between Christian and Islamic viewpoints is Christians believe that Heaven is open only to people who accept Jesus Christ as their saviour. Muslims believe Jesus was one of 120,000 prophets and Mohammad is the final prophet, sent by God, to remind people why He created them, and what He expects in return.

The difference between Muslims and Christians is that Muslims believe everyone is born pure, whereas the Christians believe all are born sinful. God created humans because He wanted to share with us the bounties and benefits of existence. He gave each the unlimited potential to be realised during a lifetime. When the soul is resurrected having discovered its true nature, it will face a compassionate and loving God. Those who have forgotten why God created them and had ignored their responsibilities, will come into the presence of a severe and wrathful God.

No two people are alike, and everyone needs God's (Allah's) guidance in finding their paths. Finding and remaining on one path requires discipline, adherence to the laws of personal and spiritual conduct outlined in the Koran, and constant nurturing of one's connection with the creator. Almighty God is unknowable, and His will is made known to Muslims, who seek it and understand that everything is ultimately connected to Him.

The inter-world is where the soul goes after answering certain questions put to them by two angels when they arrive in their graves. Depending on the person's answers depends on their destination on the day of judgement. Either the Garden of Paradise or the Fires of Darkness where they are forever separated from their creator.

It's interesting to note the similar beginnings of Zoroastrianism, Judaism, and Christianity. Zoroaster, Abraham and Moses all had visions. They all wrote about the laws they were given in their visions.

Zoroastrianism, Judaism, Christianity and Islam, all have very similar beliefs about the one God: He is the creator and He is omnipresent (is everywhere).

Both Christianity and Islam believe in Judgement day. All the monotheistic religions believe in good and evil and accept the presence of a God, and an adversary some call the Devil, or Satan, etc. who is always trying to undermine the good done in the world and who lives not in heaven but in hell.

Magic & Demons

While there is no explanation for gargoyles, we do know that artisan as far back as the Bronze Age used the grotesque, gorgons, sphinxes and griffins to avert the powers of evil from buildings. Most of the gargoyles and grotesques in Gothic architecture are copied from pre-Christian deities that may still have exerted a substantial control over the people of the Middle Ages. The Celt Empire covered most of modern-day Western Europe in the years just before Christ was born, and the Gothic iconography in the Middle Ages was from Celtic beliefs. The gargoyles and grotesques are mainly deities of the Celts from stories that were passed on in folk tales and whose likenesses remained talismans of luck and protection. The church recognising the impossibility of completely supplanting such rich religious tradition tolerated the images with uncharacteristic tact and forbearance. Because of this even today we can see these gargoyles on churches and cathedrals as well as large ancient buildings.

As long as man has worshipped gods etc. he has accepted the possibility of malevolent spirits. His way of dealing with them was at first to try and appease them through gifts, prayers, rituals and sacrifice, and when that didn't work, he made up magic, potions, and incantations. He also used mythical creatures to defend against evil and often carried lucky charms for personal protection. If these didn't protect him, he would call on someone practised in the art of magic to help.

In 5000 BC in ancient Mesopotamia, the Sumerian people feared malevolent forces. In their religious thinking, the concept of evil spirits embraced both demons and ghosts of the dead. At funerals, if the deceased were dissatisfied with the quality of the food and drink given as funeral offerings, they would return from the underworld, to lurk in corners and graveyards and sometimes even enter houses. Those who died violent deaths were especially likely to come back and seize the living entering their bodies through the ear. Particular spirits also caused certain diseases, which had to be treated by professional exorcists. A large body of magical incantations grew to combat demons and ghosts as well as witches.

Cylinder seals were sometimes used to work counter-magic against hostile magic that was practiced by witches both male and female. One of green stone, for example, was twirled while the counter attacker said: "O witch, like the twirling of this seal, may your face spin and turn green."

The witches made images of their victims, but this method could be used against them by way of a series of magic rituals that were known as burnings, because many of them involved burning the image of the witch while chanting incantations.

Ancient Mesopotamians regarded curses as physical things that could enter the human body. If a curse was suspected the victim would hire an exorcist to diagnose the cause, possibly a bad deed or something done unwittingly. For instance, if the patient had "disrespected his parents, injured his neighbours or drunk from the cup of a person under a curse". After the diagnosis, the exorcist handed the patient an onion, a date, a bit of matting and some tufts of wool. These the victim pulled to pieces one by one and threw them into the fire while reciting an incantation. "Like this onion that I peel and throw in the fire, so may, guilt, sin, wickedness, transgression, and the pain that is in my body be peeled off," and so on.

Mesopotamian exorcists used transference magic only. If a child had a fever, they recited a particular incantation three times, rubbed the infant from head to foot with a loaf of bread, and then threw the bread to a dog. In theory, this ensured that the fever transferred from the child to the dog. For every fear, it seems they found a creative solution.

Black magic, spells, curses, possession, illness, convulsions, mental problems, etc. were all considered the work of evil. Prayers, magic charms, potions, fasting, torture, transference magic, spells, sacrifice, drowning, rituals, iconology, holy water, etc. were all dreamed up to combat the forces of evil. With the passing of time, it has become apparent disease is not the work of the Devil any more than mental problems. No doubt in the future, causes of possession and the different types of mental problems, and curses, as well as ghosts and hauntings, will be better understood. Until that day, people will rely on outdated methods (which rarely worked) to deal with things they don't understand. An example is mental illness; drugs treat the symptoms, yet the causes are ignored. The cause can be a chemical imbalance or defects in the brain. It could also be interference from outside the brain, by spirits influencing people's thoughts through the mind. Haunting of people and houses is still mostly believed to be the work of evil entities, yet some good ghosts/spirits may not know they are interfering with someone's life or mind. Sometimes spirits are confused, and their very presence can affect sensitive people, just by being in the same vicinity their aches and pains can be felt.

Witches & Demons

During the years, 400 BCE to the 1500th-century, superstition was rife in the known world, and because of the decline in some religions and rise in others, there was no consistency in how to deal with the beliefs of the ordinary people. Persecution and execution of witches have been going on since ancient times and continues today in some parts of the world. The Romans passed laws that had a provision against evil incantation and spells. In 331 BCE, 170 women were executed as witches in the context of an epidemic illness it was thought they were responsible for. In 184 BCE, about 2000 were killed for witchcraft. In 182–180 BCE, another 3000 executions took place, again, triggered by an outbreak of an epidemic. It wasn't only the Romans who persecuted witches; it was happening all over the ancient world. In the Roman Empire, witches continued to be persecuted until the 4th century.

In the early Middle Ages, The Catholic Church tried to check the fanaticism about witchcraft and necromancy in the decrees of the Council of Paderborn, which explicitly outlawed accusing people as witches, and if a witch was burned, whoever burnt them were put to death. This law conforms to the teachings of Canon Episcopi of 990

ADS, and the thoughts of Augustine Hippo, which stated that witchcraft did not exist and that to teach that it was a reality was a false and heterodox teaching. In 794, the Council of Frankfurt was also clear when censuring the harassment of suspected wizards and witches. The Council also said it was superstitious to believe in witchcraft and the penalty for anyone who burnt witches was death. King Kalman of Hungary banned witch-hunting because he said witches did not exist.

That witches did not exist was the general opinion of more enlightened leaders until about 1320, when Pope John XXII authorised the Inquisition to prosecute sorcerers (although inquisitorial courts rarely dealt with witchcraft except when investigating heterodoxy). There are many Catholics who preached against witchcraft. One was Bernardino of Siena, whose sermons preached against superstitious practices and an over-reaction towards spells and enchantments by the ordinary people.

In the Middle Ages religion was dominated by Christianity. It was during this time they built cathedrals in Europe, and the Catholic Church started universities in Paris, Tubingen, Cambridge, and Oxford. The only church in Europe was the

Catholic Church, and the church leaders like Bishops and Archbishops controlled the laws set out by the government as they held all the leading roles in the government. It was a time when the power in the hands of the Pope was so great that he could even excommunicate the King for a misdeed. The general population was dominated entirely by the church all their lives and many religious institutions gained power and wealth. During the 12th century, large cathedrals were built to accommodate the increased population, as Roman style churches became inadequate.

A network of Christian monasteries had sprung up as monks and nuns were forbidden the right to own property, leave the monastery or get involved in worldly concerns and desires. Monks and nuns of this era were well educated; they devoted their entire lives to learning and writing. The knowledge and education of the classical world were preserved in the monasteries. The early Middle Ages also saw a considerable increase in missionary activities. Christianity spread by Missionaries to many parts of the world helped to bring various cultures together.

During the Middle Ages, Christianity was the leading religion and attempts to purify the church and society resulted in many Christian campaigns against other faiths. These campaigns controlled by bishops, scholars, and warriors, made efforts to make the Christian world free of all non-Christians. Included in these attacks were Jews, Muslims, Pagans, and Gypsies. Jews, being considered the greatest threat to Christianity suffered the most. The highest power during the Middle Ages was the Roman Catholic Church, which was a stabilising force in everyday life, and kept the community framework together. Public policies in the governance of the people were all affected by religion including the rules and laws of the land. Any threat by other faiths to Christianity was rejected with force, and all means were taken to extend the Christian faith to other parts of the world. The society of the day was superstitious and uneducated and believed in what the religious institutions taught them.

In the 13th century, Thomas Aquinas was instrumental in developing the new theology that would give rise to the witch hunts. But because secular courts judged sorcery and not heresy, it was not until Maleficarum that heresy was a crime for which theological trials for witchcraft could commence. The resurgence of witch hunts coincided with some developments in Christian doctrine, for example, the recognition that witchcraft was a form of satanic influence and its classification as heresy. As Renaissance occultism gained traction among the educated classes, the belief in witchcraft that was part of folk religion of the uneducated rural population was integrated into a progressively all-embracing theology of Satan as the ultimate source of all Maleficarum.

Many of these mythologies were brought over and adapted from the paganism of the barbaric tribes that over the centuries converted, and became Christians in the Middle Ages. Because of the Christian dogmatic theology, every ancient religion and their gods, were considered superstitious practices that served demons. As the population held the belief in demons, it wasn't difficult to accept that demons could take different forms and identities, with which to taunt and injure people. What is remarkable is how often European tales speak of religious objects as a means of warding off such creatures. Often these were the metaphors for how Christianity was more powerful than the old gods of the pagan practices. The more ancient mythologies speak of potions and protective words, and pagan throwbacks. Consequently, people that tried such things were associated with paganism and labelled as witches and warlocks since even good charms had to come from the Devil. Furthermore, the frailty of life with sickness, famine, war and death, which was a very close reality, meant they didn't live to a great age. In the Middle Ages, there were many miracles performed by sinners and saints. Although many in the modern world may scorn at some of the deeds, many thousands saw incidents like raising the dead, healing, strange victories and defeats, and weather shifting. Fledgling science was mixed with superstition involving incantations and special ingredients since the knowledge was not there to think success could be achieved otherwise.

Middle Ages

In the Middle Ages, the Catholic Church disapproved of any kind of divination or fortune telling. Necromancy was regarded with horror. The dead might choose to appear in dreams, but they must not be summoned by the living for their own purposes. Those who practiced necromancy were often members of the Christian clergy though some non-clerical practitioners are known. In some instances, apprentices or those ordained to lower orders dabbled in the practice. They were connected by the belief in the manipulation of spiritual beings, especially demons practicing magic. Those involved were almost always literate and well educated. Most possessed basic knowledge of exorcism and had access to texts of astrology and demonology. Clerical training was informal, and university-based education was rare. Many were trained as apprentices and were expected to have a basic knowledge of Latin, ritual, and doctrine. This education was not always linked to spiritual guidance and seminars were very rare. The situation allowed some aspiring clerics to combine Christian rites with occult practices, despite its condemnation in Christian doctrine.

These practitioners thought three things would be achieved with Necromancy. The manipulation of the will, knowledge and illusions.

Manipulation of the will affects the mind and will of another person, animal or spirit. Demons are summoned to cause various afflictions on others, "to drive them mad, to inflame them to love or hatred, to gain their favour or to constrain them to do or not do some deed".

Illusions involve conjuring food or reanimation of the dead, a mode of transportation or entertainment.

Knowledge is supposedly provided when demons give details about different things. This might be by identifying criminals, revealing the whereabouts of certain items or information about the future.

Performing medieval necromancy usually involved magic circles, conjuring's and sacrifices. Circles were often traced on the ground, and various objects, shapes, symbols, and letters may have been drawn or placed within to represent a mixture of Christian and occult ideas. Circles were believed to protect and empower what was contained within, including protecting the necromancer from conjured demons.

Conjuration is a way of communicating with the demons to help them enter the physical plane. Select words and stances are used, and the power of these words and stances, as well as Christian prayers of biblical verses, are used to call the demons. These may be repeated in succession or to different directions until the summoning is complete.

Sacrifice was a payment for summoning, although it may be the flesh of a human or an animal, it could sometimes be as simple as offering an individual object.

These practices were common place during these troubled times as people sought cures for illnesses and control of others in their lives. Although the above discusses the clergy, there were many men, and women, who were herbalists, or local wise women who were considered witches. Priests, monks or women, were often responsible for looking after the sick and dying.

After the 12th century, the spread of university education produced a new class of trained male doctors. Many patients preferred the practical skills of the local wise woman to the theoretical learning of the university educated male physicians. Midwives were particularly valued, but during the 1420s, English doctors tried to get parliament to ban all uneducated healers and specifically women, from medical practice, but parliament refused. The Pope supported the doctors and was particularly anxious to suppress midwives. Several decades later the witch-hunter's handbook, Malleus Maleficarum, declared that no one did more harm to the Catholic faith than midwives, stating that when they did not kill and eat new-born babies, they dedicated them to the Devil.

Published in 1487, The Malleus Maleficarum (The Hammer of Witches) was the most popular handbook for witch hunters during the 16th century. Although banned by the church in 1490, it was used during the Renaissance and contributed to the brutal prosecution of witchcraft in the 16th and 17th centuries. It was written by a German Catholic clergyman Heinrich Kramer in 1486. It was reprinted in 14 editions and by 1520 had become unduly influential in secular courts. Jacob Sprenger, also a clergyman, is said to be a co-author, but it is thought his name was used to add official authority to the work. They were prosecutors of heretics in Germany. In 1490 the Catholic Church condemned the work and there were protests about their behaviour to Pope Innocent VII, who had recently been elected.

The Malleus gave theological approval to every gross superstition concerning diabolism and witches and resulted in thousands of innocent people being tortured and put to death, particularly women. Witches supposedly exercised great power over the sexual act and were often held responsible for causing inappropriate infatuations, impotence and sterility. Cementing the pact with the Devil usually involved sexual intercourse, as well as eating new-born babies and making ointments out of their remains. Once the contract was made, the witches' magical acts, such as sprinkling water to produce rain or injuring a wax image of a person, were a sign to the demons, who then made the intended event happen. The witch's familiar, or demon, helped her in everything. Accused witches were tortured until they confessed. But the Malleus also recommended their confessions be obtained by promises of mercy, not mercy for the witch, but for the society whose best interest was served by the destruction of the witch. People who believed such promises and confessed to witchcraft were invariably disappointed. Witchcraft went into decline in the 15th and early 16th centuries before becoming a major issue again and peaking in the 17th century. Previously, the belief that some people possessed supernatural powers now became a sign of a pact with the Devil. To justify the killings, Protestant Christianity deemed witchcraft as being associated with wild ritual parties that were satanic in nature with naked dancing and cannibalistic infanticide. It was considered as heresy for going against the first of the Ten Commandments (You shall have no other God before me) and from Exodus 22:18 "Thou shalt not suffer a witch to live".

There were around 40,000–50,000 people executed during witch trials in Europe. Although the last witch trial in England was in 1711, the Witchcraft Act wasn't repealed until 1951 and revised by the Fraudulent Mediums Act. The last person convicted under the Witchcraft Act was Jane Rebecca Yorke in September 1944 for pretending that spirits of deceased persons to be present, and she was bound over.

The Fraudulent Mediums Act was repealed on 26th May 2008 and replaced by the Consumer Protection Regulations following an EU directive regarding unfair sales and marketing practices.

There are still numerous people being executed or burnt as witches around the world today.

The "Middle Ages" are not unique for their superstitions and mythology. There has yet to be a race of human beings that has not produced or embraced a set of superstitions of fables. While such things helped explain the unknown, it was seldom comforting, filling the unknown with mysterious beings that were, even more, threatening.

Witch hunts still happen today in cultures where magic is still believed. In many cases, they are acts of hanging and burning, reported quite regularly from parts of sub-Saharan Africa, from rural North India and Papua New Guinea. Also, some countries continue to legislate against practicing sorcery. The only country where witchcraft remains legally punishable by death is Saudi Arabia.

Witch hunting in modern times are continuously reported by the UNHCR (United Nations High Commission for Refugees) of the UNO (United Nations Organisation) as a serious infringement of human rights. Although many of those blamed are women and children, elderly people and marginalised groups of the community such as HIV infected and albinos are also accused. These suspects are considered a burden to the society, resulting in them being driven out, starved or violently killed, often by their own families in an effort of social cleansing. The causes of witch hunts include poverty, epidemics, social crisis and inadequate education. Those conducting the witch hunt are usually a leader in the community or witch doctor. They could also receive a payment, by charging for an exorcism or sometimes selling parts of the murdered remains. In many communities of Sub-Saharan Africa, the fear of witches drives periodic witch hunts in which specialists are called in to identify the suspected witches, resulting most often in death by a mob. Countries specifically affected by this phenomenon include South Africa, Cameroon, The Democratic Republic of the Congo, and many African countries.

The BBC reported witch hunts against children in 1999 in the Congo and Tanzania, where the government responded to attacks on women accused of being witches for having red eyes. A woman in Ghana launched a lawsuit in 2001, where witch hunts are also common when she was charged with being a witch. In Africa relatives seeking the property of the accused often lead witch hunts against them.

It also goes on in Asia, where in India condemning a woman as a witch is not uncommon to grab land, settle scores or even to punish her for turning down sexual advances. In the most cases, the accused is either forced to abandon her home and family or driven to commit suicide. Most incidents are not documented because it is difficult for poor and illiterate women to travel from isolated regions to file police reports. In 2010, it was estimated the number of women killed as witches in India was between 150 and 200.

In Papua, New Guinea, the practice of white magic such as faith healing is legal and the 1976 Sorcery Act carried a penalty of up to two years in prison for practicing black magic until it was repealed in 2013. The accusations and deaths from being accused as a witch were still happening in June 2013, when four women were accused of witchcraft and tortured because the family had a permanent house made of wood, had good educations and a high social standing. One of the women was beheaded.

Witchcraft or sorcery remains a criminal offence in Saudi Arabia, although the precise nature of the crime is undefined. Most of those accused of witchcraft are beheaded and, while it is not known how many, the last that we know of was in June 2012.

We can see from the above the belief in witchcraft, sorcery and black magic, which would include demons the Devil and Satan, are still rife today. It's very common in the African and Asian communities for exorcists to be employed to remove curses, illnesses, and spells.

The world today is as vulnerable to superstition and mythology as it has always been. In fact, a case could be made that the modern world is obsessed with such things, just as much as any other period of history. Blocks of flats and hotels as well as office blocks are still built without a 13th floor. Leaders of countries from ancient times to modern times including presidents and prime ministers are known to have consulted astrologists before making important decisions. Newspapers contain horoscopes, and people consider success or failure to be dependent on whether they have carried out certain routines, or worn favourite clothes, lucky objects or words. Our mythology now is featured in comic books and TV shows depicting people with astounding abilities, heavenly bodies, and impossible wealth. Many would say that we know such things aren't real; yet if one combines surgeries, special devices, drugs, and foods, dietary programs, seminars, etc. we are looking at billions of pounds and hours spent in the pursuit of our gods and goddesses, without considering how much is spent on therapy for failing to live the dream.

Summary

I've tried to show how humankind has through lack of understanding attempted to control his environment with ancient deities and gods. By using deceased ancestors, gods, spirits and supernatural agents, as explanations for births, deaths, catastrophic floods, solar and lunar eclipses, abundance or scarcity of food, the rising and falling of tides and tribal defeats of victories, and a variety of other occurrences that are no longer mysteries, the object has been to see why humankind has the belief in ghosts, angels, demons, the Devil and many more mythical entities.

The idea that there is only one God linked with the division of the soul and the body developed into one of the most influential methods of controlling the masses ever seen. This culminated in people having to behave themselves for two reasons: one, for the well-being of the society; and the other, was for their personal well-being for all eternity.

I have considered some of the beliefs about the afterlife of some of the world's major religions. I have tried to show how religions have evolved in ways that enabled people to adapt their situations and make sense of their lives. The evolutionary process is ongoing, beliefs come and go as other beliefs take their place. This, as we have seen, takes time, and the process can be extremely tedious.

It's clear to see how the rise of the agricultural society changed man's perception of his place in this world and the next.

There are millions of people who believe their version of God is correct, and that their path to eternal life is the only pathway. All other versions and pathways are wrong to the extent that anyone who does not believe as they do, are the enemies of God.

Many Greek philosophers had significant input into the present-day beliefs in the supernatural.

The name of Satan comes from the Hebrew and means adversary, or the Arabic shaitan meaning astray, distant, and sometimes Devil. This figure first appears in the text of the Zoroastrian religion under the name Angra Mainyu, who brings evil and temptation. He is known as the deceiver who leads humanity astray and is also called the Devil who possesses demonic qualities.

The name Devil is from the Greek diabolos = slanderer or accuser and is considered in most religions, cultures, and beliefs to be a supernatural entity that is the personification of evil and the archenemy of God and humanity.

It's clear to see how demonic entities would be used to control the populations once one God was accepted as the Supreme Being. The community could no longer contact their God directly; it had to be done via a priest or holy man. This gave great power to the representatives of the religions of the day. By realising they could go to a dark, unwelcoming place if they did wrong, and a beautiful warm and light place if they were good, the population was much easier to control. We must remember that the religious leaders had the ear of the ruling elite and could change or direct belief as they saw fit. So, by conjuring up a nasty frightening future for the wrong doers, they could control large amounts of people. They also called demons and malevolent entities to control people in this life making them fear a visit from evil spirits if they didn't live following Gods word i.e. do what the priests told them.

Spirits are just dead people, nothing more, and the only way they can influence you is through the mind, where the imagination builds on the thoughts that are projected. Yes, spirits are real, and there are good and not so good, a person doesn't necessarily change when they die. They can and do affect your thoughts if you are not aware of what is and isn't your own. They are not mystical beings but ordinary people who have died, and who may be suffering in some way. Imagine if you expected to go to heaven and you didn't arrive, you would be very upset and possibly fearful of what comes next. After all, you've been told about hell and damnation; if you're not in heaven, you must be in hell. It's interesting to note that the idea of heaven and hell is accepted because history propagates the idea, but no mention so far of a place where souls can get lost.

BOOK TWO

Different Religions & Beliefs

The following is an excerpt about different religions, how they perceive ghosts and hauntings, and how they deal with them.

Extract fromWiki-how.com

Exorcism (from Greek ἐξορκισμός, *exorkismos* – binding by oath) is the religious or spiritual practice of purportedly evicting demons or other spiritual entities from a person or an area they are believed to have possessed. Depending on the spiritual beliefs of the exorcist, this may be done by causing the entity to swear an oath, performing an elaborate ritual or simply by commanding it to depart in the name of a higher power. The practice is ancient and part of the belief system of many cultures and religions.

Buddhism

Nature of ghosts

Tibetan Buddhists believe that when a person dies, they enter the intermediate Bardo state from which they may be reborn in this world in a human or animal body, in the ghost world in a ghost body, in one of the paradise realms, or one of the hells. Eventually, however, the person will die in this after-death world and be reborn as a human or other creature unless they achieve Nirvana, where they are beyond all states of embodiment.

Hungry ghosts have their own realm depicted on the Bhavacakra and are represented as teardrop or paisley-shaped with bloated stomachs and necks too thin to pass food, so that attempting to eat is also incredibly painful. Some are described as having "mouths the size of a needle's eye and a stomach the size of a mountain". This is a metaphor for people futilely attempting to fulfil their illusory physical desires. Sometimes individuals have a predominance of hungry ghosts in their makeup. They can never get enough, and are always hungry for more. The Tibetan word for the emotional state of the hungry ghost, *ser na*, literally means "yellow-nosed", and could be said to mean "meanness" or "lack of generosity". The person in this state is constantly seeking to consume and to enrich themselves, but can never be satisfied.

A Tulpa is a type of ghost or being that is created through mental effort, purely from the thoughts of its creator. A very skilled Buddhist practitioner or sorcerer may have this ability, and in some cases, a Tulpa may be created from the collective thoughts of the villagers. Such a ghost is not self-aware at first, but may gradually acquire awareness and go on to become a normal human being.

Dealing with ghosts

Phurba

The Phurba (Tibetan ཕུར་བ, Sanskrit: *kīla*) is a ritual dagger used by a tantric practitioner to release an evil spirit from its suffering and guide it to a better rebirth. Such a spirit (ghost) is a being which lingers in confusion between different realms. By plunging the dagger into it, it is thrown out of its confusion and gets the chance to be reborn, probably as a lower kind than human.

Spirit traps

Families often mount ghost-traps on the roofs of their houses; spindle-like contraptions wound with coloured yarns. A spirit trap may also be hung in a tree. The series of interlocking threads is thought to ensnare the spirit and is burnt when the job is done.

Exorcising-Ghost day

The Tibetan religious ceremony "Gutor" {དགུ་གཏོར་}, literally offering of the 29th, is held on the 29th of the 12th Tibetan month, with its focus on driving out all negativity, including evil spirits and misfortunes of the past year, and starting the New Year in a peaceful and auspicious way.

The temples and monasteries throughout Tibet hold grand religious dance ceremonies, with the largest at Potala Palace in Lhasa. Families clean their houses on this day, decorate the rooms and eat a special noodle soup called Guthuk. In the evening, the people carry torches, calling out the words of exorcism.

Christianity

The examples and perspective in this section may not include all significant viewpoints.

In Christianity, exorcism is the practice of casting out demons. In Christian practice, the person performing the exorcism, known as an exorcist, is often a member of the Christian Church, or an individual thought to be graced with special powers or skills. The exorcist may use prayers and religious material, such as set formulas, gestures, symbols, icons, amulets, etc. The exorcist often invokes God, Jesus and several different angels and archangels to intervene with the exorcism. A survey of Christian exorcists found that most exorcists believe that any mature Christian can perform an exorcism, not just members of the clergy. Christian exorcists most commonly believe the authority given to them by the Father, Son, and Holy Spirit (the Trinity) is the source of their ability to cast out demons.

In general, people considered to be possessed are not regarded as evil in themselves, nor wholly responsible for their actions, because possession is thought to be unwilling manipulation by a demon resulting in harm to self or others. Therefore, practitioners regard exorcism as more of a cure than a punishment. The mainstream rituals usually take this into account, making sure that there is no violence to the possessed, only that they are tied down if there is potential for violence,

Catholic

In Catholic Christianity, exorcisms are performed in the name of Jesus Christ. A distinction is made between a formal exorcism, which can only be conducted by a priest during a baptism or with the permission of a Bishop, and "prayers of deliverance", which can be said by anyone.

The Catholic rite of a formal exorcism called a "Major Exorcism", is given in Section 11 of the Rituale Romanum. The Ritual lists guidelines for conducting an exorcism, and for determining when a formal exorcism is required. Priests are instructed to carefully determine that the nature of the affliction is not a psychological or physical illness before proceeding.

In Catholic practice, the person performing the exorcism, known as an exorcist, is a consecrated priest. The exorcist recites prayers following the rubrics of the rite and may make use of religious materials such as icons and sacramentals. The exorcist invokes God – specifically the Name of Jesus – as well as members of the Church Triumphant and the Archangel Michael to intervene with the exorcism. The Catholic understanding is, several weekly exorcisms over many years are sometimes required to expel a deeply entrenched demon.⸱

In general, possessed persons are not regarded as evil in themselves, nor wholly responsible for their actions. Therefore, practitioners regard exorcism as a cure and not some kind of punishment. The Catholic rite usually takes this into account, ensuring that there is no violence to those possessed, only that they are tied down if deemed necessary for their protection and that of the practitioners.

History

In the 15th century, Catholic exorcists were both priestly and lay, since every Christian was considered as having the power to command demons and drive them out in the name of Christ. These exorcists used the Benedictine formula: "Vade retro Satana!" ("Step back, Satan!") By the late 1960s, Roman Catholic exorcisms were seldom performed in the United States, but by the mid-1970s, popular film and literature revived interest in the ritual, with thousands claiming demonic possession. Maverick priests who belonged to right-wing fringes took advantage of the increase in demand and performed exorcisms with little or no official sanction. The exorcisms that they performed were, according to *Contemporary American Religion*, "clandestine, underground affairs, undertaken without the approval of the

Catholic Church and without the rigorous psychological screening that the church required. In subsequent years, the church took more aggressive action on the demon-expulsion front". In 2014, the Roman Catholic organisation, International Association of Exorcists, received the approval of the Vatican.

When an Exorcism is required

According to the Vatican guidelines issued in 1999, "the person who claims to be possessed must be evaluated by doctors to rule out a mental or physical illness". Most reported cases do not require an exorcism because twentieth-century Catholic officials regard genuine demonic possession as an extremely rare phenomenon that is easily confounded with natural mental disturbances. Many times, a person just needs spiritual or medical help, especially if drugs or other addictions are present. After the need of the person has been determined then the appropriate help will be met. In the circumstance of spiritual help, prayers may be offered, or the laying on of hands or a counselling session may be prescribed.

Signs

Signs of demonic invasion vary depending on the type of demon and its purpose, including:

1. Loss or lack of appetite.
2. Cutting, scratching and biting of skin.
3. A cold feeling in the room.
4. Unnatural bodily postures and change in the person's face and body.
5. The possessed losing control of their normal personality and entering a frenzy or rage, and attacking others.
6. Change in the person's voice.
7. Supernatural physical strength not subject to the person's build or age.
8. Speaking or understanding another language which they never learned before.
9. Knowledge of things that are distant or hidden.
10. Prediction of future events (sometimes through dreams).
11. Levitation and moving of objects/things.
12. Expelling of objects/things.
13. Intense hatred and violent reaction toward all religious objects or items.
14. Antipathy towards entering a church, speaking Jesus' name or hearing Scripture.

Process of the Exorcism

In the process of an exorcism the person possessed may be restrained so that they do not harm themselves or any person present. The exorcist then prays and commands for the demons to retreat. The Catholic Priest recites certain prayers and follows procedures listed in the ritual of the exorcism revised by the Vatican in 1999. Seasoned exorcists use the Rituale Romanum as a starting point, not always following the prescribed formula exactly. *The Gale Encyclopedia of the Unusual and Unexplained* describes that an exorcism was a confrontation and not simply a prayer and once it has begun it must finish no matter how long it takes. If the exorcist stops the rite, then the demon will pursue him, which is why finishing the process is so essential. After the exorcism, has been finished the person possessed feels a "kind of release of guilt and feels reborn and freed from sin". Not all exorcisms are successful the first time; it could take days, weeks, or months of constant prayer and exorcisms.

On this subject, there is the 2009 book by journalist Matt Baglio called *The Rite*, which inspired the film The Rite.

Notable Examples

1928 – Emma Schmidt underwent a 14-day exorcism performed by Catholic priest Theophilus Riesinger. There are no records apart from information on Theophilus Riesinger. 1949 – Roland Doe was allegedly possessed and underwent an exorcism. The events later inspired the novel and film The Exorcist. The 1973 film The Exorcist was based on the book of the same name by William Peter Blatty, published in 1971 which was in turn based on the exorcism in 1949 of Ronald Doe (a pseudonym). It was a sensation, scaring cinema audiences with its horrifying content. It tells of a 12-yeard-old girl, who was supposedly possessed by the Devil and how her family contacted their pastor for help.

This is what is supposed to have happened as far as can be discovered:

Roland was born into a German Lutheran family, and during the 1940s the family lived in Cottage City, Maryland. He was an only child who depended on adults in his family for playmates, mostly his aunt, Harriet. Aunt Harriet was a spiritualist, and she introduced Roland to the Ouija board when he told her of his interest in it.

After his Aunt's death, the family experienced strange noises, furniture moving of its own accord and ordinary objects flying or levitating when Roland was nearby. The family became concerned and turned to their pastor for help. The pastor, long interested in parapsychology, arranged for the boy to stay overnight at his home so that he could observe him. When parapsychologist J.B. Rhine learned that the pastor claimed he had witnessed household objects and furniture seemingly moving by themselves, he wondered if he unconsciously exaggerated some of the facts. The pastor advised Roland's parents to see a Catholic priest.

According to the traditional story, Roland underwent a number of exorcisms performed by Edward Hughes, a Roman Catholic priest at Georgetown University Hospital, a Jesuit institution. During one session of exorcism, Roland allegedly slipped one of his hands out of the restraints, broke a bedspring from under the mattress and slashed the priest's arm, which resulted in the exorcism being halted.

The family travelled to St Louis to see Raymond J Bishop, a professor at Roland's cousins University. The professor spoke with an associate William S. Bowdern at College Church, and together they went to visit Roland at his relative's home. They allegedly observed a shaking of the bed, flying objects, and the boy speaking Latin in a guttural voice, and exhibiting an aversion to anything sacred. Bowdern was granted permission from the archbishop to perform another exorcism.

Before the exorcism ritual began, another priest, Walter Halloran, was called to the psychiatric wing of the hospital, where he was asked to assist Bowdern. William Van Roo was also asked to assist. Halloran stated that words such as "evil" and "hell", along with various other marks, appeared on Roland's body. During the Litany of Saints portion of the exorcism ritual, the boy's mattress began to shake, and Roland broke Halloran's nose during the process when he lashed out. Halloran told a reporter that after the rite was over the boy went on to lead an ordinary life.

It's been suggested by today's experts that Roland was just a deeply disturbed boy, and there was nothing supernatural about him.

It's also suggested that Roland was simply a disturbed bully who threw deliberate tantrums to get attention or to get out of school. Halloran says he never heard the boy's voice change and that he thought he merely mimicked Latin words he heard the clergymen say, rather than a sudden ability to speak Latin. When marks appeared on Roland's body, the priests failed to check the boy's fingernails to see if he had made the marks himself. There are also questions as to whether Hughes' arm was slashed by a bedspring as no evidence of the incident could be found. A suggestion was made that the priests were influenced by their own expectations.

To psychiatrists, Roland suffered from mental illness. To priests, this was a case of demonic possession. Those involved saw what they were trained to see yet it doesn't explain how Roland went on to lead an ordinary life. If he had a mental illness did it, just go away?

The above is the basis for the film The Exorcist, however, in the film, Roland was changed to a girl. The levitation and crawling across the ceiling, head spinning and pea soup episodes were dramatisations added to the book and film.

The Exorcism of Emily Rose

Taken from Wikipedia.org

The Exorcism of Emily Rose and Requiem were films based on a real exorcism of a German woman called Anneliese Michel. She underwent 67 exorcisms between 1975 and 1976. In a conference, several years later, German bishops retracted the claim that she was possessed. Here's what is supposed to have happened:

When Anneliese was 16 years old, she experienced an epileptic seizure and severe convulsion and was diagnosed with temporal lobe epilepsy. She was diagnosed as depressed and treated at a psychiatric hospital. When she was 18, she suffered a third seizure at the psychiatric hospital where she was staying. She was prescribed anti-convulsion drugs for the first time, including Dilantin, which didn't bring immediate relief. She began hallucinating while praying at various times of the day, and complained about hearing voices telling her she was damned and would "rot in hell". That same month she was prescribed another drug, Aolept, which is like Chlorpromazine, which is used to treat various psychoses including Schizophrenia and disturbed behaviour, in her case spiritual delusions.

The treatment didn't improve her health, and she became more depressed. By the time, she was 20 years old, she had become intolerant to various religious objects, including a crucifix, and refused to drink holy water. Despite medication, she got worse, and became suicidal. Being a devout Catholic, Anneliese grew increasingly frustrated with the medical intervention and she and her family were convinced demons possessed her.

They consulted with several Catholic priests for an exorcism. The priests declined and recommended the continuation of medical treatment and informed the family that exorcisms required the bishop's permission.

In the Catholic Church, official approval for an exorcism is given when a person strictly meets the set criteria. They are then considered to be suffering from possession and under demonic control, intense dislike for religious objects and "supernatural powers" are some of the first indications. The condition of Anneliese worsened physically, and she began displaying aggression, self-injury, drank her urine and ate insects. In 1973, she was put on Tegretol, an anti-seizure drug and mood stabiliser. She continued taking anti-psychotic drugs during the religious rites until shortly before her death.

The family met with a priest Ernst Alt, who on seeing their daughter declared that "she didn't look like an epileptic" and that he did not see her having seizures. He believed she was suffering from demonic possession and urged the local bishop to allow an exorcism. In September of the same year, Bishop Josef Stangl granted the priest Arnold Renz permission to exorcise following the Ritual Romanum of 1614 (the 1999 update of the Rite can be found on Wikipedia), but ordered total secrecy. Renz performed the first session on 24th September, and her family stopped seeking medical treatment and relied solely on the exorcism rites. The sessions lasted up to four hours and were repeated at a rate of one or two each week, a total of 67 sessions were performed over a period of ten months. Anneliese began talking increasingly about "dying to atone for the wayward youth of the day and the apostate priests of the modern church" and refused to eat towards the end.

She died in July 1976, and the autopsy report stated the cause of death was malnutrition and dehydration because of being in a semi-starvation state for almost a year while the rites of exorcism were performed. Both her knees were broken due to the continuous genuflections (dropping to her knees) and she was unable to move without assistance and it was reported she was suffering from pneumonia as well. After the investigation, it was reported that her death could have been prevented even one week before she died if she had been given medical attention. The case has been cited as an example of misidentified mental illness, negligence, abuse and religious hysteria.

In 1976 the state charged Anneliese Michel's parents and two priests Ernst Alt and Arnold Renz with negligent homicide. The accused were found guilty of manslaughter resulting from negligence and were sentenced to six months in jail (which was later suspended) and three years of probation. The prosecution concluded that the parents should be exempt from punishment as they had suffered enough. The case has been labelled as a misidentification of mental illness, negligence, abuse and religious hysteria.

During the trial, doctors testified that Anneliese was not possessed but stated this was a psychological effect because of her strict religious upbringing and her epilepsy. As we can see the film is very loosely based on the actual case, nothing as dramatic happened. I wonder what would have happened if a medium had been present during the original diagnosis.

2015 – On May 20th, 2015, the Catholic Church secretly carried out a ritual of exorcism at San Luis Potosi Cathedral for the entire country of Mexico. Its purpose was to help put an end to the ongoing Drug and Cartel War in the country, which had already claimed over 60,000 lives. It was the first ever Catholic exorcism of an entire country. Several members of the church took part in the ceremony, which was intended to end the high levels of violence, drug cartels, and abortion in the country. The exorcism didn't focus on any one individual but rather an entire country, which is a highly unusual move for a ritual that is unconventional to begin with.

One priest involved in the exorcism, Father Fortea, said, "…to the extent, sin increases more and more in a country. To that extent, it becomes easier for the demons to tempt (people)." He warned: "…to the extent, there is more witchcraft and Satanism going on in a country, to that extent there will be more extraordinary manifestations of those powers of darkness."

Father Fortea said that, "The exorcism performed in San Luis Potosi is the first ever carried out in Mexico in which the exorcists came from different parts of the country and gathered together to exorcise the powers of darkness, not from a person, but from the whole country.

"This rite of exorcism, beautiful and liturgical, had never taken place in any part of the world. Although it had taken place in a private manner as when Saint Francis (exorcised) the Italian city of Arezzo," he stated.

The Spanish exorcist explained, "The celebration of this ritual will not automatically change the difficult situation Mexico is going through in a single day.

"It would be a big mistake to think that by performing a full-scale exorcism of the country everything would automatically change right away."

Nevertheless, he emphasised: "If with the power we've received from Christ we expel the demons from a country, this will certainly have positive repercussions because we'll make a great number of the tempters flee, even if the exorcism is partial.

"We don't drive out all the evil spirits from a country with just one ceremony. But even though all will not be expelled, those that were removed are not there anymore."

Father Fortea stressed that, "When the exorcists of a country drive out its demons, it has to be done in faith. You're not going to see anything, feel anything, there's not going to be any extraordinary phenomenon. We have to have faith that God conferred on the apostles a power, and that we can use this power."

In any case, if the ritual were to be carried out in more countries once a year before or after, this would put an end to any extraordinary manifestations that would show us the rage of the Devil. Because, without a doubt, the demons hate to be driven out of place or to be bound with the power of Christ.

The Spanish exorcist said, "It would be very desirable that when there's an annual meeting of exorcists in a country, a ritual such as this Exorcismo Magno that took place in Mexico be performed."

He also stressed that a bishop "can authorise its occurrence once a year with his priests in the cathedral".

It's interesting to see they need to perform the ritual of exorcism many times on a weekly basis on an individual to see any progress, yet for a whole country once is enough, or even once a year. In neither case was there any evidence of success.

I wonder where they think the demons go. To a adjoining country or to hell? It would be nice to see some improvement then they could do the same for the rest of the world on a regular basis. I don't say positive thinking is wrong; I think it can move mountains. I just question why they don't consider the possibility that some of these demons could be lost souls crying out for help.

Hinduism

The image of Hanuman at the Hanuman temple in Sarangpur is said to be so powerful that a mere look at it by people affected by evil spirits, drives the evil spirits out of them.

Beliefs and practices about the practice of exorcism are prominently connected with Hindus. Of the four Vedas (holy books of the Hindus), the Atharva Veda is said to contain the secrets related to exorcism, magic, and alchemy. The basic means of exorcism are the mantra and the vajna used in both Vedic and Tantric traditions. Vaishnava traditions also employ a recitation of names of Narasimha and reading scriptures, notably the Bhagavata Purana aloud.

According to Gita Mahatmya of Padma Purana, reading the 3rd, 7th and 9th chapter of Bhagavad Gita and mentally offering the result to departed persons helps them to get released from their ghostly situation. Continuous playing of mantras, keeping scriptures and holy pictures of the deities (Shiva, Vishnu, Hanuman, Brahma, Shakti, etc. especially of Narasimha) in the house, burning incense offered during a Puja, sprinkling water from holy rivers, and blowing conches used in *puja* are other effective practices.

The main puranic resource on ghost and death-related information are Garuda Purana.

A complete description of birth and death and about the human soul are explained in Katō Upanishad, a part of Yajur Veda. A summary of this is also available as a separate scripture called Kāttakaṃ.

Islam

In Islam, exorcism is called *ruqya*. It is used to repair the damage caused by *sihr* or black majic. Exorcisms today are part of a wider body of contemporary Islamic alternative medicine called *al-Tibb al-Nabawi* (Medicine of the Prophet).

Islamic exorcisms consist of the treated person lying down, while a sheikh places a hand on a patient's head while reciting verses from the Quran.[1] The drinking of holy water (Zamzam Water from Zamzam Well), may also take place.

Specific verses from the Quran are recited, which glorify God (e.g. The Throne Verse in Arabic, and invoke God's help). In some cases, the adhan – "ah-zan" – the call for daily prayers, is also read, as this has the effect of repelling non-angelic unseen beings or the jinn.

The Islamic prophet Muhammad taught his followers to read the last three suras from the Quran, Surat al-Ikhlas (The Fidelity), Surat al-Falaq (The Dawn) and Surat al-Nas (Mankind). The trend in *al-Tibb al-Nabawi* treatments, cosmetic and toiletries is often associated with fundamentalists who charge that Western, chemically laced prescriptions aim to poison Muslims or defile them with insulin and other medicines made from pigs.

Members of terrorist groups have been involved in Islamic remedies as healers and sellers, while some clinics are used as recruiting grounds for Islamist causes. Islamic medicine carries a cachet that, by taking it, you are reinforcing your faith and the profits go to Muslims. According to Sydney Jones, an expert on Islam in Southeast Asia with the International Crisis group, there were two court cases in Belgium in 2012 and England also in 2012 set out below, which will give you some idea of a radical treatment of exorcism in modern times.

In 2012, six people stood trial in a Belgian Court for the 2004 murder of a young Muslim woman in a deadly act of exorcism. Her body was found covered with bruises, and her lungs filled with water. The detainees in the case included two self-appointed exorcists, the victim's husband and three female members of a radical Muslim Group. Later, her husband admitted to investigators that his wife was subjected to month-long sessions of exorcism to evict from her body the demons that prevented her from becoming pregnant. During this period, according to Belgium media reports, the young woman had swallowed litres of holy water. She was fed two spoons of yogurt every day and always had earphones playing the verses from the Quran. To evict the demons, the exorcists reportedly put their fingers down her throat and forced her into bathing in hot water and beat her with a stick.

Also, in 2012, a British Court convicted three men of assault and causing actual bodily harm after they had beaten a female member of the family they believed showed signs of demonic possession. She was beaten for almost eight hours in January 2011. A fourth suspect remains at large.

Judaism

Josephus reports exorcisms performed by administering poisonous root extracts and others by making sacrifices. The Dead Sea Scrolls mention that exorcisms were done by the Essene branch of Judaism.

In more recent times, Rabbi Yehuda Fetaya authored the book *Minchat Yahuda*, which deals extensively with exorcism, his experience with possessed people, and other subjects of Jewish thought. The book is written in Hebrew and was translated into English.

Rabbi Gershon Winkler explains that the procedure for a Jewish exorcism is intended not only to drive away the possessing force but to help both the possessor and the possessed in the act of healing. The Jewish exorcism ritual is performed by a rabbi who has mastered practical Kabbalah. Also present is a minyan (a group of ten adult males), who gather in a circle around the possessed person. The group recites Psalm 91 three times, and then the rabbi blows a shofar (a ram's horn).

The shofar is blown in a certain way, with various notes and tones, in effect to "shatter the body" so that the possessing force will be shaken loose. After it has been shaken loose, the rabbi begins to communicate with it and ask it questions such as why it is possessing the body of the possessed. The minyan may pray for it and perform a ceremony for it to enable it to feel safe so that it can leave the person's body.

Shamanism

Hypotheses on origins

Shamanic practices may originate as early as the Paleolithic, predating all organised religions, and certainly as early as the Neolithic period. The earliest known undisputed burial of a shaman (and by extension the earliest undisputed evidence of shamans and shamanic practices) date back to the early Upper Paleolithic era (c. 30,000 BP) in what is now the Czech Republic.

Sanskrit scholar and comparative mythologist Michael Witzel, proposes that all the world's mythologies, and the concepts and practices of shamans, can be traced to the migrations of two prehistoric populations: The Gondwana type (of circa 65,000 years ago,) and the Laurasian type (of circa 40,000 years ago,). The more recent Laurasian types of myths and forms of shamanism are found in Eurasian and North and South America. They are later cultural elaborations based upon the earlier Gondwana types of myths and shamanism, both of which probably derived from an earlier human source population. Witzel argues that survivals of the older, original forms of shamanism are therefore to be found in the southern hemisphere among peoples such as the San Bushmen of Botswana, the Andamanese of the Andaman

Islands off the coast of Burma, and the Aborigines of Australia. The so-called "classical" shamanism of Siberia and the Americas reflect a further cultural evolutionary development at the local levels.

Early anthropologist studies theorise that shamanism developed as a magic practice to ensure a successful hunt or gathering of food. Evidence in caves and drawings on walls support indications that shamanism started during the Paleolithic era. One such picture featured a half-animal, with the face and legs of a man, with antlers and a tail of a stag.

Archaeological evidence exists for Mesolithic shamanism. The oldest known shaman grave in the world is in the Czech Republic at Dolni Vestonice (National Geographic No 174 October 1988). This grave site was evidence of a female shaman.

In November 2008, researchers from the Hebrew University of Jerusalem announced the discovery of a 12,000-year-old site in Israel that is perceived as one of the earliest known shaman burials. The elderly woman had been arranged on her side, with her legs apart and folded inward at the knee. Ten large stones were placed on the head, pelvis and arms. Among her unusual grave goods were 50 complete tortoise shells, a human foot, and certain body parts from animals such as a cow tail and eagle wings. Other animal remains came from a boar, leopard, and two martens. "It seems that the woman... was perceived as being in a close relationship with these animal spirits," researchers noted. The grave was one of at least 28 graves at the site, located in a cave in lower Galilee and belonging to the Natufian culture, but is said to be unlike any other among the Epipaleolithic Natufians or in the Paleolithic period.

Robert Sapolsky has theorised that shamanism is practiced by schizotypal individuals.

Beliefs

There are many variations of shamanism throughout the world, but several common beliefs are shared by all forms of shamanism. Common beliefs identified by Eliade (1972) are the following:

- Spirits exist, and they play important roles both in individual lives and in human society.
- The shaman can communicate with the spirit world.
- Spirits can be benevolent or malevolent.
- The shaman can treat sickness caused by malevolent spirits.
- The shaman can employ trance inducing techniques to incite visionary ecstasy and go on vision quests.
- The shaman's spirit can leave the body to enter the supernatural world to search for answers.
- The shaman evokes animal images as spirit guides, omens, and message-bearers.
- The shaman can perform other varied forms of divination, scry, throw bones/runes, and sometimes foretell of future events.

Shamanism is based on the premise that the visible world is pervaded by invisible forces or spirits which affect the lives of the living. Although the causes of disease lie in the spiritual realm, inspired by malicious spirits, both spiritual and physical methods are used to heal. Commonly, a shaman "enters the body" of the patient to confront the spiritual infirmity and heals by banishing the infectious spirit.

Many shamans have expert knowledge of medicinal plants native to their area, and herbal treatment is often prescribed. In many places shamans learn directly from the plants, harnessing their effects and healing properties, after obtaining permission from the indwelling or patron spirits. In the Peruvian Amazon Basin, shamans and curanderos use medicine songs called icaros to evoke spirits. Before a spirit can be summoned, it must teach the shaman its song. The use of totemic items such as rocks with special powers and an animating spirit is common.

Such practices are presumably very ancient. Plato wrote in his *Phaedrus* that the "first prophecies were the words of an oak", and that those who lived at that time found it rewarding enough to "listen to an oak or stone, so long as it was telling the truth".

Belief in witchcraft and sorcery, known as *brujería* in Latin America, exists in many societies. Other societies assert all shamans have the power to both cure and kill. Those with shamanic knowledge usually enjoy great power and prestige in the community, but they may also be regarded suspiciously or fearfully as potentially harmful to others.

By engaging in their work, a shaman is exposed to significant personal risk, from the spirit world, from enemy shamans, or from the means employed to alter the shaman's state of consciousness. Shamanic plant materials can be toxic or fatal if misused. Failure to return from an out-of-body journey can lead to death. Spells are commonly used to protect against these dangers, and the use of more dangerous plants is often very highly ritualised. From the above, we can see that shamans enter the spirit world to remove invading spirits who are causing illness or distress.

Spiritualism

Spiritism says that people and animals that have been loved (had their vibrations raised) such as pets, continue to live after physical death. On crossing over we take three things with us: our etheric or spirit body (a duplicate of our physical body), memories and character.

On crossing, we go to a realm that will accommodate the vibrations we accumulated from all the thoughts and actions of our lifetime. Average decent people go to what is usually termed as the "Third Realm". Those who have been willfully cruel and consistently selfish go to the darker, very unpleasant astral regions because their level of vibrations would be much lower than the vibrations of the "Third Realm".

Information transmitted from the other side tells us that the "Third Realm" is a place of enormous beauty, peace, and light. There will be scope to continue to spiritually refine indefinitely. Those who earned it can progress to the fourth level, then the fifth, and sixth and so on. For humans, we know that there are at least seven realms vibrating from the lowest to the highest vibration – the highest vibrations being more beautiful and with better conditions.

Spiritualists accept the law of progress that those who are in the lower realms will one day slowly go upwardly towards the Realms of the Light, even if it takes eons of time.

Unlike all other religions which require faith and belief, (faith in a belief without evidence), spiritualism is the only religion which is based on evidence and direct experience. Spiritism briefly is very like spiritualism and is based on Alan Kardec's research.

Spiritualism is the acceptance of empirically elicited evidence that the human consciousness survives physical death and that those who survive can communicate with those who are physically on earth in a number of ways. This communication can be made through at least 20 different empirically validated processes including mental, physical and direct voice mediumship, telepathy, xenoglossia, electronic voice phenomena, instrumental trans-communication, apparitions, Ouija Board, death bed visions, and poltergeists.

Also, spiritualists follow the universal law of cause and effect, accepting self-responsibility and that the universe is governed by mind, commonly called God.

The modern spiritualist movement began in 1848 in Hydesville, New York, with the Fox sisters who demonstrated that spirits communicated with them by rapping on tables. The historical record is the finding of a skeleton in the basement where the Fox sisters used to live. The spirit of a man who was murdered there directed the Fox sisters to search by digging in the basement. The finding of the skeleton confirmed the rapping's directed at the two Fox sisters. The murdered former resident of the house informed the Fox sisters who murdered him and the police caught the murderer.

Today, as it has been for thousands of years, millions of people around the world experience communication from their loved ones who are in the afterlife. Communication is now accepted worldwide, and highly credible world famous scientists using their scientific skills regularly confirm this communication. Scientific testing is being done regularly on gifted mediums with great success; some spiritualists organise themselves and have service meetings in spiritualist churches, while others call themselves spiritualists without aligning to any formal organisation.

Possession

Demonic Possession is not an accepted psychiatric or medical condition recognised by either the ICD-10 or the DSM-V. Those who have a belief in demonic possession have occasionally credited to the condition the symptoms of mental or physical illnesses, such as hysteria, mania, psychosis, Tourette's syndrome, epilepsy, schizophrenia or dissociative identity disorder.

Also, there is a type of monomania called demonopathy or demonomania where the patient believes they are possessed by one or more demons. The illusion that some people who are experiencing symptoms of possession and that exorcism works are attributed to the placebo effect and the power of suggestion. Sometimes people act demonically possessed to gain attention; it is suggested they are narcissists or are suffering from low self-esteem.

Psychology

We see from the history of spirit possession and exorcism how the phenomenon has become a reality in many people's minds. Blatant and subtle beliefs develop which threaten the existence of objective spirits interacting with the living. Though spirit possession is generally accepted as being an objective threat to humanity, it remains a solely individual experience. Historical examination shows that the social and cultural background of a civilisation defines the deviations, extent, and meaning of possession. The very experience itself is dependent upon the religious beliefs, customs, and expectations of society, as are rites of exorcism. Owing to the unpredictable changes in a society, we cannot judge who is or isn't possessed. If someone is, in his cultural environment, considered to be in a state of spirit possession, then he, or she is possessed.

Those who believe in voodoo accept the possessing spirit enters the head of the victim and displaces the person's soul. In the West, malicious spirits usually attach to the victim's aura causing various disturbances, which can lead to total possession. The zar spirit – is believed to have originated in Ethiopia, in the Middle East and the Sudan, is sometimes referred to as sar – mainly possesses women who are experiencing domestic conflict, yet appears to leave after the woman's needs have been satisfied. Spirit possession ebbs and flows depending upon the current belief system operating within a community. Specific subgroups are prone to possessing spirits, repeatedly seeking them out within a population. For example, lonely, isolated or depressed people are particularly prone to interference or possession. Within societies where spirit possession is endorsed, it is often used as a last resort for people within these subgroups to gain attention and get their needs met. The situation is that spirits which are central to one subgroup in multiple societies are marginal to other units within the same system. For example, when Christians and pagans lived side by side, the pagans thought the idea of possession in Christian belief quite absurd.

The belief in possession is a prerequisite for the existence of entities that interfere with the living. It's simple if a person doesn't believe in the possibility of being possessed, they won't experience possession by outside entities, whether the spirits be evil or inspirational. Where belief in possession is high, discarnate spirits are busy possessing individuals and cause all sorts of mayhem in that society. In places around the world, if one believes in possession by a demon or god, the entity will often behave as if it's that demon or god that has been called. If an exorcist has certain beliefs, they can also directly shape the experience of possession for the possessed. An exorcist intending to speak to the possessing spirits is much less likely to come up against the traditional demonic behaviours of hissing, convulsions, foaming at the mouth, and screaming obscenities as is the exorcist who believes he's doing battle with the forces of hell. It's the exorcist's beliefs that often play a large part in the deciding factor in decisions about possession, either by a person thinking themselves possessed or bothered by psychic forces, or by an investigator or other outside observers.

In the West, spirit possession is one of the most powerful spiritual experiences a person can encounter. It's the contact with an outside force and the feeling of being taken over by forces that cannot usually be recognised. An energy that maliciously tries to inflict pain, harm, and torture to its victim. Possession by a spirit is a subjective phenomenon that often becomes overwhelming due to the objectified individual interpretation by the victim. Many people who encounter poltergeist or PK activity in their home attribute the strange occurrences to an evil spirit. It is evil because it is the unknown; it is an objective entity, since a person cannot believe that the mind can affect matter. The strange phenomena almost immediately cease once the agent (the person whose mind is creating the disturbance) is known, and psychological issues addressed. It's accepted that beneath the attack of entity attachment will be found something within the person that has allowed the possession to occur (Auebach 1993).

The ability of spirits to possess the living receives validation through the supernatural occurrences that usually accompany the possession. Spirits who communicate with the living through mediums regularly provide certain facts relating to individuals in the audience that the medium could not possibly have known. This extraordinary ability creates the assumption that there must be a spirit coming through from the spirit realms, particularly in situations where a deceased relative gives details that only a family member would know. During WWI and WWII, public interest in spiritualism and theosophy increased because it claimed to give people the chance to communicate with deceased loved ones. It is rare for people who experience a medium's unique talents to consider alternative explanations. The super-psi or super-ESP hypothesis states that it's the psychic abilities of the living person (in this case the medium) who is accessing the information (details of the deceased person's life), thus creating the impression that the discarnate soul is speaking (Auerbach1986). The medium may be unknowingly receiving information from a member of the family who is still living who would know the factual details; psi abilities are unimpeded by time and space. Recent studies into the effects of magnetic fields suggest that information may be locked in the environment itself. Multiple personality disorders Schizophrenia and MPD are occasionally linked with spirit possession. In MPD, the individual accepts the identity of more than one person. The characters can be very different alleging they are of a different race, gender, age, and family. The level of intelligence between the various personalities has been known to change; each identity has a distinct personality profile, and personality specific mental disorders may also occur. MPD is a severe form or psychological disassociation. The history of childhood incest, torture, or other abuses are found in 95% to 100% of MPD cases. Personalities are linked to past traumatic episodes. Each separate personality retains the person's age, characteristics, and emotional mood at the time of the traumatic event and they are stuck or frozen in the incident. Schizophrenia is distinctly different from MPD, since psychotic symptoms and delusional thinking is associated with schizophrenia. Existing in a reality where they can put thoughts into the heads of others, and other people can implant thoughts, and experience hallucinations are typical characteristics of schizophrenia. While it may be appealing to associate multiple personalities as being discarnate spirits, the history of each personality coming from the individual's past makes the spirit possession hypothesis unlikely.

Being possessed by discarnate spirit serves a few functions in our society. Those who firmly believe they are possessed believe the only way to be cured is with an exorcism. It's often considered as a last resort for those undergoing obstinate psychological disorders. More commonly it operates as a type of mental disassociation. Deep, upsetting psychological material doesn't have to be accepted by the victim if they adopt the ideology of spirit possession. That means we don't have to be accountable for the conditions in our community where crime, violence and other types of evil breed. The devil can be blamed for that as well. So, I think it's a counsel for irresponsibility for genuine emotional, physical and psychological problems where exorcism can easily be considered as a quick fix.

A massive amount of investigation has been done on the effects of excessive stress. During WWII, numerous soldiers developed battle neuroses, including shell-shock. A severe case of shell-shock caused by the terrifying experiences of warfare (even today), culminated in emotional and mental overload, making the individual withdraw completely from their surroundings, locking them into an inner reality of terror, where they were unable to function or relate to the outer world. Drugs such as ether and Methedrine were given to help create the situation of deep emotional excitement that often leads to a state of emotional catharsis. The intense emotional release was the primary agent facilitating recovery. Exorcisms function, in the same way, as the tried and tested method of curing the possessed and getting rid of unwanted spirits that have invaded them. The above follows the same sort of pattern as our drug abreaction treatments of battle neuroses. The patient who is possessed is worked up into a state of frenzied emotional excitement, in which they express intense anger and fear. That usually leads to collapse, which is followed by a calm feeling and release from the entity that has been tormenting them, just as our patients felt released from traumatic memories. The underlying processes of exorcism also have much in common with mesmerism. The subtleties of spirit possession show peculiarities as well. The person who fears the devil is close to him will suddenly start to feel with complete certainty that the Devil is really in them and possessing them. The same mechanism is behind sudden feelings of possession by God, of God dwelling within one or becoming part of God.

In a lecture given by William James in 1896, he spoke about his investigation into the psychology of spirit possession and talked about demonic possession. Expanding on a previous address in which he gave three kinds of alternatives to the personal sense insanity, hysteria, and somnambulistic, he added to this lecture a 4th: spirit possession or mediumship. In reply to the refusal of the scientific community to consider this

4th mutation he wrote: "That the demon theory will resurface again is to my mind certain." He also believed that if there were demons, the only way they could enter an individual would be through a cracked or broken self. Most importantly, he suggested the mind is a system of ideas, which produce diverse compositions based on new ideas through a process of expansionism and stagnation. He quotes Professor Leaba's conclusion that, "The ground of the specific assurance in religious dogmas is then an effective emotional experience. The objects of faith may even be unusual; the effective stream will flow along, and invest them with unshakable certitude. The more startlingly effective the experience, the less explicable it seems, and the easier it is to make it a carrier of unsubstantiated ideas." This description offers profound insight into the enthusiastic acknowledgment of spirit possession, as well as the mysterious powers observed in the ritual of exorcism.

The psychological processes of the individual concerned with spirit possession are critical to understanding the experience. Psychological factors are discussed in the Spirit Releasement Therapy, Technique Manual that inadvertently brings the ideas of spirit possession and rational explanations much closer together. William J. Baldwin's observation that "most attached spirits do not make their presence known to the host", (Baldwin 1991) is indicative of how the subconscious mind typically operates. He goes on to elaborate: "Entities seem to function at the level of the unconscious." A clear directive that spirit possession is psychological in origin will be in his book. The attached entity is functioning within the level of the subconscious mind of the host. The urges, attitudes, likes and dislikes, appetites and behaviours of the entity seem to blend with the clients own. No evidence exists that indicates possessing spirits are not of the subconscious mind. Parapsychologist Lloyd Auerbach explains: "There's nothing to connect the demon with reality, and certainly nothing that says that the new personality isn't some monster from the Id, from the subconscious." (Auerbach 1993) The psychology of Carl Jung provides a spacious container for considering the psychological elements involved with spirit possession. Rather than exiling the experience to the basement of the unconscious, labelling it a neurosis, Jung offers a more profound explanation. He sees possessing spirits directly related to archetypes and warns,

"The chief danger is that of succumbing to the fascinating influence of the archetypes, and this is most likely to happen when the archetypal images are not made conscious. It may even happen that the archetypal figures, which are endowed with a certain autonomy because of their numinosity, will escape from the conscious control altogether and become completely independent, thus producing the phenomenon of possession." (Jung 1959) Interestingly many of the causes of spirit possession, (prolonged fatigue, harbouring negative emotions, alcoholism, drug use, depression, stress) are the very causes that allow for the content of the unconscious mind to influence the conscious mind. Since a lot of unconscious thoughts are not owned by the individual, it will most likely be perceived as an incredibly negative existence: from the outside. Describing the events that initiate demonic possession is highly accurate, except that the demon originates from within. There are times when we must battle entities and demons whether we like it or not.

The rites of exorcism and spirit possession are seldom equated with an altered state of consciousness (ASC). It's unfortunate since research done in altered states can assist in explaining how and why spirit possession occurs. It's known that ASC can cause a change in perception; an altered perception produces a change in a person's reality. The increased susceptibility characteristic of ASC is useful in understanding exorcisms and their effectiveness. Because exorcisms make use of techniques that alter the consciousness, like hypnosis, emotional fervour, and ecstatic dance, is no surprise. Being possessed by a spirit is a subjective phenomenon that feels as though it is experienced objectively. Although the person may know the demons are within the body or mind, he/she is totally unidentified with them, and they are experienced as alien objective intruders. The state of possession usually would not be a person's ordinary waking state, although this can occur. ASC is related to earthbound spirits, demons, spirit possession and exorcisms.

Spirit Releasement Therapy (SRT), practiced by a trained therapist within the context that includes traditional therapy also, functions as a therapeutic tool available for integrating deep unconscious shadow material. Material deemed so wretchedly vile by the person's psyche requires initial work at integration must assume the form of dissociative storytelling. Past life regression therapy operates in a much similar manner, yet there is greater owning of the contents of the stories by the person. The practice of SRT can also pose serious threats to both therapist and client, since literal interpretation by either will likely result in a potentially severe distortion of reality. The client convinced that he/she is possessed, or has been possessed, may begin to view events in life as a cause of evil demons inflicting unjust punishments. Personal baggage is thrown on to the discarnate beings and is no longer owned by the client. Personal responsibility is in jeopardy of extinction. As a therapist, one finds in their patients that which they both expect to find. Freud began to speculate that women suffered a mental illness due to childhood molestation from their fathers. Upon testing the hypotheses, he discovered every single one of his female patients was molested by their fathers. Freud soon realised that due to his suggestions he was responsible for the findings. Consequently, therapists who are trained in SRT discover that in their practice new patients as well as old patients, are suddenly showing signs of possession/recall as if the clients and entities were waiting for the therapist to learn the techniques

(Baldwin). If both the therapist and client are caught up in the story, there is little hope that long-term results will follow and eventually, another spirit is bound to attach itself to the patient. The insight and understanding that can unfold through SRT will be a lost treasure, remaining hidden in the hidden complexities of the mind.

Exorcism and Mental Illness

Psychosurgery has been described as "Neurosurgical Exorcisms" by one scholar, with trepanation (boring holes in the skull) having been widely used to release demons from the brain. Meanwhile, another scholar has equated psychotherapy with exorcism. It's important to make sure any person claiming to be troubled by ghosts has no history of psychological problems. Many of the symptoms associated with hauntings can be experienced by someone with psychiatric or psychological problems. Even when a person is diagnosed with mental illness, there will be spirits around who can also be affecting their feelings. It's not always easy to remove the interference as they won't know whether it's the drugs or spirits that are causing their anxieties. A medium will be aware of the spirits but even if they are removed it will make no difference to the individual suffering with mental problems or side-effects from medication. They may still have the effect of the drugs in their system, which can be causing a chemical imbalance to the brain. These drugs are very powerful and can damage the brain beyond recovery; the original reason for them taking the drugs may have been ghostly interference. Once on this mind changing medication, it's a long road to weaning themselves off, and until they have, there is little chance of resolving the interference they are experiencing from discarnate spirits if at all.

The Medium's Point of View

The preceding chapters give you a taste of beliefs from many religions and what they believe will protect them from discarnate spirit. What did you think? Now apply that same reasoning from a spirit's point of view; are their beliefs going to affect you the spirit? These rituals and remedies are based on belief from the physical perspective, not spirits. Yes, the haunting spirits were on the earth at some time, but once they acclimatise themselves with their new surroundings, the physical world no longer affects them. They can move by just a thought, and their senses are no longer restricted by the heavy physical body or dense vibrations of the physical world. They are energy with no weight or restrictions and can transmit and intercept thoughts as we can the spoken word. Once they have passed over and are settled in the spirit world, they learn that all humanity originated from the same place. This knowledge makes them think twice about the religious beliefs they had, and the effect it has is diminished by this greater understanding of the reality that they now exist in. If you as the spirit don't believe in mankind's religions, why would you be affected by words spoken in a ritual or prayer? The only time a departed spirit would be affected is if they were still earthbound and still believed in the faith they had when on the earth plane. When dealing with haunting spirits, it's important to establish their understanding of where they are. They can then be treated depending on their knowledge and belief. For example, if I have been in the spirit world for a while and I am fully acclimatised to my surroundings, I will be aware of the spirits around me and the earth plane as well as the reality of my existence. Therefore, I will not be affected by prayers and rituals such as holy water, candles, burning of herbs or ringing of bells, neither would the mention of a religious icon or deity have any effect.

I know that physical and religious ceremonial icons, symbols and prayers, are not going to stop me doing what I'm doing. There is only one way to stop me, and that is by someone stronger than me from the spirit realms, interceding on behalf of the person or people I am haunting or interacting with. That's why some mediums can remove discarnate spirits who are causing problems. They are in communication with their spirit workers or guides and work as a team from both sides of the veil. On the earth plane to educate the haunted and help them to understand how and why they are being attacked. In the spirit world to remove the offending spirit by their spirit helpers.

Some mediums will talk to the misguided spirit and apply logic and understanding as to why they should stop what they're doing, and show them the way back to their loved ones in the spirit world. Others will just send them to the light, which won't always work because they're trusting the spirit will obey. It's always better to take the spirit to the light as then the medium will know they have been removed. All work done when removing haunting spirits should be done with intent, as it is the intention and co-operation of the spirit world that gets the job done.

The biggest problem is the person who is being haunted. There is a multitude of reasons why a house won't be cleared, and the main one is the occupants. If they are living alone and want attention because of loneliness, then any attention is better than none. They don't have the willpower to move out of their loneliness, so if they're getting attention and interaction in any way from spirit, they will accept it. Other times they have trouble believing the spirit has gone and are constantly looking to see if they have. That, of course, helps them to stay tuned to the spirit world, and they will get what they're looking for. Many times, when I've visited haunted houses with the purpose of clearing them, I've found there's been some traumatic occurrence before the haunting began. This trauma has opened their senses, and because they have become more sensitive, they are tuning into the spirit world that they otherwise would not have noticed. Drugs or alcohol can alter the perception of the individual by numbing the brain, and the person is unable to control their thoughts and actions. Drugs, whether medical or recreational, can give hallucinations and subdue the thought process, and this can lead to people losing control, and their brain will be open to spirit interference through the mind. Once that connection is made it's not always easy to close it again. There are many millions of people who go through life without getting any spirit interference or do, and don't recognise it. They just put it down to life's hiccups and let it go. It's only when they're persistently bothered that they begin to question what's happening.

Sometimes determination and perseverance will help with the removal of unwanted spirit, but you need a strong mind to overcome doubts. Often when the spirit is still focused on the earth plane and retains their religious beliefs, prayers, and attributes, we can use their beliefs to persuade them to move on. They're often removed from one place and end up bothering someone else, because they have been dealt with as if they are evil, rather than lost or misguided. Many of these lost souls are just crying out for help, but some religions consider them evil and "cast them out" somewhere. Other religions erect spirit traps to catch the spirits and then burn the traps. Unless the spirit believes, this will have no effect on them, just as salt across the thresholds of windows and doors will not stop them. If in life holy water and the burning of candles, prayers or the use of salt or other symbols had no effect on you, why would it when you're in spirit? I have touched on some of the better-known religions and the way they exorcise spirits, but there are many more different ways and beliefs. While I point out the reasons why these rituals and remedies may not work I will say that sometimes they do. That is because the intent and belief are there and even without the ability to communicate with spirit, they will occasionally step forward and help. It is my belief that everyone has guides in the spirit world, which although maybe unknown, will still intercede if the intent is strong enough. That is why the same ritual performed by one person may work and when another person performs it, it doesn't. The placebo effect can also work if you believe in something enough, it will happen.

Performing an exorcism or rescuing lost souls is not a game and can be very dangerous if not done in the right way. It's not something to aspire to; it chooses you. It can possess your life if you don't have the proper protection so if you don't have to, don't get involved. It's imperative that you can close yourself down from spiritual things, and negative energies, and live as normally as possible when you're not working in this way. There's no glamour in this work, and if you're not adequately protected, there is only misery and interference and you become a target for those who want to disrupt people's lives. If you try to interfere when someone is being haunted, they will attack you to frighten you off. They may even transfer their aggression to you, so if you decide to get involved be entirely sure, there's no other way. Many are the times I have visited someone to find they've had someone come to remove the spirits. The trouble is if it wasn't done properly, things got worse. So, it's not just your life but the people you are attempting to help who will suffer if it's not done correctly.

There are many lost souls in the spirit realms and often they are the cause of most hauntings. They're not malicious or vindictive, they're just trying to ask for help. So, once we've helped them find peace, the people being haunted find they no longer get interference. There's always more than one, and we've found people who've visited the house before us, have assumed that only one spirit is there. By asking them to go to the light, they think the job is done. We've found many spirits still around the house feeling frustrated because they thought they were going to get help, but they weren't noticed. They may try to attract attention to their plight again or resign themselves to their situation. It's only because of the belief by the medium or exorcist that only one spirit is causing the problem. Also, if the spirit is malicious, the exorcist must understand who or what they're dealing with and work accordingly. Otherwise, the job will be left unfinished. When they say, things can get worse, it's true, as the offending spirit thinks they're invincible and can get nasty, because the spirits believe they can't be stopped. That is why it's so important to know what you're doing in these situations. Don't get involved unless you have no other choice, and if you do, then learn as much as you can before you expose yourself to the dangers of exorcisms done badly. Make no mistake, you will be attacked at some point, and if you can't defend yourself, they can make your life a misery.

Understanding Hauntings

The question that one should ask first is who or what is haunting and why... whether it is a discarnate spirit or a problem of the brain or mind? There is a responsibility of the person who is to carry out the removal of the spirit to first ascertain that it is a discarnate spirit causing the problem. There are many different beliefs as to what and who invades people's consciousness and homes, the following just a few. There are issues with health and side effects from medication, belief in black magic and curses, departed spirits that have unfinished business, natural phenomena, like noises in the house and dark energies, ghosts, poltergeists, demons, aliens, etc. Quite often it's thought that someone who lived or died in the house is responsible, or the ground is haunted by past events. Any of these can be the reason, so it's important to know what you're dealing with before you start. Most of the preceding are manifestations from the spirit world; they will work on your sensitivity or weakness to get a reaction.

The history of the individual asking for help will usually point the exorcist, or conducting religious representative, in the right direction as to what is happening. If it is decided that a haunting is taking place, then the preparations can be made for whatever rituals, prayers and procedures considered necessary are instigated. Each religion has a way of dealing with departed spirits and interestingly they are not all the same. It's dependent on the belief and doctrine of the religion as described in their holy books. The view ranges from malevolent spirits who should be cast out, to lost spirits who are seeking comfort and assistance to move on. Some religions don't believe in evil, just not so good, or not so bad, and that the departed spirit needs guidance and healing. Others believe there are aliens who come to frighten people, or dark energies are being sent to cause mayhem. Whatever the belief it's becoming more common all over the world to ask for help in dealing with hauntings. Since the 1950s, there has been a 50% increase in these requests in the Western world, although it's commonplace in the Eastern world. Before this, people didn't like to talk about their problems because they might be considered delusional or just plain crazy. Many people feared being diagnosed as mentally ill and being institutionalised. Or being shunned by their church or circle of friends, fearing they may be contaminated. Sometimes these people were avoided and in some cultures feared as being in league with the devil. Other cultures revered these individuals and treated them as special because they were in touch with their ancestors. There is no consistency across the religions, and because of this, there are so many different ways of dealing with discarnate spirit. During the years, I have been working in this field I have only come across intelligent spirits who either don't know they are affecting people or are doing it on purpose. They may try to present an image that frightens, but once you get to the basics, they're all spirit.

The afflictions can take many forms from mood changes and pains to aggression and verbal abuse by the affected person. They can sometimes hear voices telling them all sorts of nasty things and making them feel worthless and undermine their confidence. It's not just the voices they hear; they can get the feeling of paranoia and persecution. Until you have experienced or come across people who are suffering in this way, you cannot appreciate what they are going through. Sometimes it's the occasional glimpse or voice; then there are the extreme cases where the interference is constant from the minute the person wakes until they finally fall asleep. It can be a relentless attack on an individual's conscious and unconscious thoughts. Sometimes the attacks continue in dreams that will seem real. So, awake or asleep there is no let-up. This case is extreme, and there are many levels of interference right down to seeing the odd shape out of the corner of your eye. It's not all who hear voices, some get feelings of oppression or depression or feel they are being watched and have no privacy. It's not uncommon for these people to see discarnate spirits; they can and sometimes do show themselves in whatever form will frighten you most. You may get things disappearing or moved, electrical items may get switched on or off, lights may flicker, pets sometimes act strangely. Sometimes you may get mood swings that are not consistent with your feelings. Sometimes you will feel a pain, and for you, there is no reason for it, this is when you may be picking up the illness or injury of a discarnate spirit who has come close to you. It's not uncommon to get hot or cold spots around the house or strange smells or noises. Young children may see people you are not aware of (like imaginary friends). Some people see nasty looking men or women while others may see the devil or grotesque faces. When you are the only one that can see someone that others say isn't there, is it any wonder you might think you're going mad or hallucinating. Some spirits will attach themselves to an individual either because they feel an affinity with them or to try to possess them or cause them discomfort in some way. These spirits will be with a person all the time even when they leave the house. It's important to know whether the spirit is housebound or a traveller.

Not all discarnate spirits are nasty; many are just lost or confused and are waiting for someone to find them, to help them understand what has happened and take them to the spirit world. There are places where the discarnate spirit will stay quite happily without causing any problems. They may be observing for their understanding or even trying to help other spirits who are lost or suffering. Most spirits are peaceful and just trying to understand what's happened to them. But like everything, it's the troublesome ones that get noticed.

Most mediums are aware of some of their guides or spiritual helpers. These are good spirits who are there to help and educate the medium and pass on understanding, through their medium to the physical world, to inform people about the spirit world. Many mediums either do not believe in evil or nasty spirits or choose to ignore the possibility.

They focus on communication from loved ones or healing for those suffering in this world. However, there are mediums who have experienced nasty spirits and will develop their gift of mediumship for the sole purpose of helping lost spirits find their way home. They assist those who are troubled by the discarnate spirit to find peace, by removing them and taking the spirits to the light. These mediums work in close co-operation with their guides to help those who get lost during their transition to spirit. With the guides on the spiritual side and the medium on the physical, they can then deal with whatever comes up. It's no good saying prayers to a spirit who had no religion in this world as they will ignore the prayers as mumbo jumbo. It's the same with a discarnate spirit that has a different belief than the person conducting the exorcism or rescue; they will take no notice of the incantations, icons, prayers, holy water or salt as they have no belief in their potency. I have found that honest conversation and logic, along with explanations of how and why the discarnate spirit is in the predicament they are in is much more helpful. It doesn't matter which part of the world or what their beliefs are, 99% will listen and be helped. Language is no barrier as spirits work with thought and feelings; there is no language in spirit.

There are those who refuse help and will not leave, as they think they have the upper hand. That is when the guides come in and remove them forcefully if necessary. The guides will take them to a place where they can't interfere with the physical world. Through talking, restraint and patience, they will eventually help the spirit to understand their new situation. All spirits will eventually return to the light and their loved ones, regardless of how nasty they have been. Because that's where they come from and that's where they belong. It's only that they have been misguided by events in their earthly life that they have trouble adapting to their new surroundings.

There is a myriad of reasons why discarnate spirit will frequent a given location. In my experience, it is rarely because they died there. To understand the why's and wherefores I propose to explain how spirit end up where they are and look at things from the discarnate spirits perspective. I will first look at the spiritual aspect and then the "remedies" used for removing them from houses and people.

Houses and places have been haunted throughout the ages, and different religions have used many different methods to help or remove them. We will look at some of them and see how they go about it, and why some methods may not work and why some of them do.

One of the biggest problems is the belief that different cultures have about what is and isn't a spirit. For instances, many of the scientific community believe it's the mind that's causing the problem and prescribe strong medication to subdue people's thoughts. Some of the diseases that have sprung up are Schizophrenia, Bi-polar, and Multiple Personality Disorder. Not all people diagnosed are haunted; there are medical conditions and drugs which cause hallucinations and delusions, and we must be careful to recognise which is happening. Schizophrenia, for instance, is not a disease as there is no pathology for it. If you don't understand or believe in the spirit world, and their ability to interact with our minds, then you will always blame the physical for the problems that are presented. Usually, a good medium will be aware when there is discarnate spirit around causing disruption or asking for help. It's only by tuning into the spirit world that a medium will know whether it's the mind or there are spirit or spirits around.

One of the common mistakes made is that there is only one discarnate spirit causing problems. In my 35 years of removing unwanted spirits, there has always been more than one, often working together, but not always. Some may be lost or confused, and others will know what's happened to them and what they're doing.

Let me just say that almost all the films and stories have been dramatised for entertainment purposes, and some of the things portrayed are pure fiction or hallucinations.

How Do Spirits Influence Us?

Each one of us is a spirit and right now involved in a physical life; essentially, we're a spirit in a physical body. When we die, we separate from our physical body and become a spiritual energy. Then depending on our beliefs and understanding, we will either go on to heaven or stay close to the earth plane. Some souls choose to stay around the earth realm; sometimes for good reasons, and sometimes not for good reasons. It is then that an exorcist may be needed. When people die, they don't change very much; in fact, they mainly stay the same. You'll take your personality with you after you die, but nothing much changes, you are still you. Sometimes you may gravitate towards places you have lived or worked, or toward people you knew in their physical life, but not always. Most ghosts are just people who're dead and negative spirits are just negative people who're dead and continue to do negative things. Very often they attack individuals and families in their homes but rarely do they attack loved ones. They sometimes make their presence known to reassure their loved ones that they are still around. But to the average person, this can be frightening, especially if they see them or witness things being moved, and more so, if they don't believe that life continues after death. Loved ones won't harm or attack you, but their presence can cause upset or frighten you. So, if there's something in your home that you can't see but you can feel, then it may be a spirit or a loved one. You may need someone to help remove the spirit, or communicate with your loved one to help you understand why they have come. Your beliefs will dictate who you approach for help, for example, it might be someone trained in the art of releasing or removing the negative spirits from your home, place of business or your person. The attacks by negative spirits are usually emotional in nature; they're trying to affect your emotions and feelings. We all generate emotional energy, and so do spirits. We all have stories of people around us producing emotional energies, whether it be positive energies like love or negative energies such as rage or anger. We can feel those emotional energies from people around us, and we know when people are feeling negative, whether it be at work or in our living environment. As I've said, people don't change when they die, and they still generate emotional energies. Although we can't see them, we sometimes feel them when they come into our homes or place of work or are with us. They can affect us and they do; the goal of an attacking spirit is to get close to us, to our person or our homes, and change the way we act. To affect us on an emotional level, to make us feel depressed, to make us feel bad, and to make us feel angry. Sometimes they strike when we're having an argument, and they will enhance the feelings that can influence us into saying things that are hurtful. Negative spirits will come close to us, generating their negative feelings and emotions and amplifying our emotions. So sometimes our emotions are not entirely ours; sometimes things that are unseen are adding to it. That's how negative spirit attacks us; they attack us on an emotional level. They want us to feel sorry, but they don't want us to know they're there and by affecting us this way it amplifies our negative feelings. The goal is to make us feel sorry and maybe do bad things, to become angry at the ones we love, to get mad at our co-workers, to become frustrated, and to become unhappy and more depressed, instead of letting us control our emotions in the usual way. There are lots of spirits out there; everybody who is dead is a spirit, and spirits have form, they don't have physical bodies, but they do have form. They generate that form as an image, the image they wish to present, which at times can be scary and while at other times it is not.

Many mediums can see the spirits and can see the images they generate. Most people can feel emotional energies, whether they are produced by living people or spirits. They will come close, and if they are in pain, we may pick up their discomfort, so by being close to us they can persuade us that the pain is ours, by influencing the mind. Discarnate spirit can attack people and invade homes all the time, and they like being around us, sometimes we're their only reference to reality. Their goal is to disrupt the family environment or to attack individual people or get a person to do or think negative things. Most spirits are good, while some are not, just like people. The medium deals with both good and not so good spirits, and the aim is to find peace for both the spirit and the person being haunted. We all have spirit guides, good spirits that are trying to talk to us and give us guidance. Our guides speak to us using telepathy — mind to mind — and they try to give us information by thoughts to give us guidance and encouragement with our ideas. The information we're getting is positive, and the feelings we're getting are good. Sometimes we feel negative like there's something bad around us in our homes or around us personally and it may be a negative spirit trying to influence our behaviour. For those who are not trained it can be difficult to gauge where the thoughts and feelings are coming from. Sometimes you will walk into a building that feels negative; it's where there's been a lot of negative emotions, like people arguing or something bad happening there. People's feelings can affect the atmosphere of buildings. Sometimes we can go into a building, and it feels light and happy and sometimes it can feel dark and oppressive. It can be the imprint of previous occupants or just spirits occupying the empty premises.

How it Works in the Spirit Realms

A spirit will choose when they want to experience life in the physical world and what they want to achieve. They will select from amongst their friends and acquaintances, who they will ask to be their guides, depending on what they want to accomplish. Those spirits who have been invited to be a guide consider it a privilege and take it very seriously because they are taking on the responsibility of guiding the new-born in life, to achieve their goals. At the birth of a baby, they have no preconceived ideas about the physical world and its beliefs. Before being born, they will have a purpose for coming to the earth plane, and this information and all their memories will be blocked from their mind like self-imposed amnesia. It's so they can experience life with a fresh approach and don't get caught up with preconceived thoughts, and their awareness will still be of the spirit world. It is only through interaction with their surroundings in the physical world that they will become fully acclimatised with the earth plane. They are innocent of all beliefs and are like a blank page that starts getting written on from the moment they are conceived. It's a great responsibility the parents and people around a new-born have because their actions and words help to create the understanding for that child. As they grow accustomed to the voices and touch of those around them, most will gradually relinquish their awareness of the spirit world. When their life is over the reverse occurs, as they start to become acclimatised with the spirit world with the help of their loved ones, who have already passed and guides who will make themselves known in the final hours of life. This process is more complicated when the individual is on medication or mentally unaware of their surroundings because of brain malfunction, or sudden death such as an accident or heart attack. Many die without any acclimatisation because their mind is so focused on the present reality. They think when their loved ones are trying to get in touch, they're dreams or memories.

When people pass from this world, the majority have no problems and move on to the next part of their journey. It's only the few that have issues, and some reach out to those sensitive enough to be aware of them on the earth plane. It's a natural process for all humanity when they pass to leave their earthly body and revert to the spirit body. The mind is the subconscious part of our physical existence and continues to be aware after physical death. Gradually, over a period (for some it's a relatively short time) and dependent on the awareness of the individual, the mind will connect to the memories of their spirit, and they will become aware of their past incarnations. Sometimes this process can be interrupted by current thought processes, like not knowing they have passed, or they have unfinished business, or even not being ready to go. There are many reasons why people get lost in the process of passing into the spirit world.

When someone dies, it can cause them anxiety and depression, not knowing what has happened or where they are. They are still in tune with the physical world but are unable to interact with people. This will cause confusion, and when they get close to people, then any pains or emotions the spirit has, may be felt by the person they come close to. It may well be that the person will not recognise where the feelings are coming from, and pass it off as their own. We must remember the newly passed soul will sometimes be focused on the physical world as they haven't experienced the feeling of being "dead". This will cause disorientation as they are so focused on what has been normal (the physical world) for them for many years. It will not even enter their mind that things have changed and how.

They may still be aware of their aches and pains and by being close to the occupants of the house or place they find themselves in, they can inadvertently transmit their discomfort to them. They almost always don't know they are doing it; they are just coming close to either feel safe or make themselves known. It can be their way of asking for help. Imagine how you would feel with people around you who didn't know you were there. Very frustrating, especially if you didn't know what had happened to you. Sometimes when we walk into a room or are close to somebody, we can feel emotions or tension. It's no different from feeling these pains or feelings from spirit; we just aren't always aware of where it's from. That can be very frightening, and sometimes you may feel a draft or touch, and you're the only one there. How about when you put something down, and it's not there when you want it, or some ornament or picture has been moved. Add these together, and it's no wonder some people start to question their sanity. Most of the preceding is a cry for help to try to attract attention to the discarnate spirits' situation. But not all are so benign; some are evil and do things purposefully to try to scare people, and to play with their mind. Some discarnate spirits will try to scare people from their homes by making their life a living hell for them or their children.

There are discarnate spirits who know exactly what they are doing and enjoy the fear and discomfort they cause the occupants of houses etc. These are the negative ones who manipulate people's minds and feelings by imposing their will, and thoughts over the occupants. If you know it's happening, you may have a chance to fight back. But if you don't, without help you're destined to suffer whatever they may impose. Some people hear voices spoken out loud, or they can get thoughts inside their head. They may feel emotions that are not appropriate for what is going on around them; these are not their feelings. How do they know what is of their mind, and do they consider it may be coming from elsewhere? Many people don't believe in life after death and would never think they could be attacked or influenced. To them, there is nothing there, so it must be their own mind and emotions. Is it any wonder these people get depressed and seek medical help? The doctors will always look to the earthly and diagnose depending on their findings, which can be wrong, and put people on medication they don't need. It's not their fault they can only prescribe following guidelines and their experience of what has worked before. They deal with the physical, and they treat the body and the reactions they see. Psychiatrists who are supposed to know what is happening to the mind frequently blame the problem on a malfunction of the brain or stress and medicate to calm people down. They don't consider the real cause, and until they start to realise the brain and the mind are separate, they will continue to treat the symptoms and not the cause. Because medical science hasn't yet recognised what mediums and mystics have known for generations, people will continue to be misdiagnosed and medicated for the rest of their lives, suffering the side effects of the powerful drugs they are prescribed. The mind is a complicated thing, and until medical science realises that the brain and mind are not the same, they will not even begin to understand how complex it is. The brain is organic and subject to malfunction through disease and chemical imbalance. The mind is the soul or spirit and is subject to influences from other discarnate minds but not affected by disease or chemicals.

The mind is and can be controlled by reason and logic and by discarnate spirits who have stronger minds or may be more persuasive. It's difficult to resist if you don't know you are being attacked, and most of the attacks to the mind are very subtle. Once a thought has been placed in the mind, it can be reinforced over and over until it appears to have originated from inside the mind and it then becomes a reality. Once the thought becomes "real" it's tough to reject it, and it takes time and understanding to realise that it isn't real. An example of this is when you wake in the morning after having a dream, only to realise that it was in fact, only a dream, and not reality. Another instance is when we get a thought in our mind that makes us feel rejected or unloved, even if we have no grounds for feeling this way. We can build it into a reality through misunderstanding or misinterpretation, until we get clarification or reassurance that ultimately changes our thoughts. Discarnate spirits can amplify these ideas until they are as real to you as your thoughts. Until you received the extra information, your mind was made up. For instance, sometimes you will wake up convinced your partner is disloyal, but once you apply logic to the thoughts or dreams they cease to make sense. Think how it would be if your waking thoughts were constantly influenced all the time by discarnate minds. You would eventually believe your thoughts, not knowing they were not yours. That's how easy it is for a discarnate spirit to influence your thoughts, especially if you want to believe.

It's the same with religion except that most people are born into a belief where they are indoctrinated by their parents, surroundings, and culture. It's very hard to tell your parents or your peers that you don't believe as they do. It's when people get older that they start to think logically and begin to make their decisions, based on education, logic, and experience. Having said that there are also those who just believe what they are told, as they have no knowledge or ability to think outside the box. It's also surprising today how people will believe in things without any proof. There are many religious books and writings the content of which are supposed to be given by God. It's interesting to note there are many beliefs as to who and what God is. It's not for me to say, we will all find comfort in our understanding. Wars have been fought because one god is thought to be the only true God, and many have and will die because of religious beliefs. All religions teach compassion and love for others.

Why does God allow bad things to happen and let thousands of people die in famines, disease, and war? The answer is he doesn't, but we do have free will. Humanity is responsible for how and where we live our lives and how we react to any given situation. This includes our belief about what comes after this life, do we cease to exist, change into an animal or continue in another way? We are spiritual beings who belong in a very different world who can inhabit the physical world for so long as the vehicle (our body) lasts. We are aliens to this physical plane, and our natural state is energy. In our natural state, we live forever, there is no beginning or end to our existence that we know of. As a spiritual energy, we are still able to interact with the physical plane through the mind and energy. Everything is made up of energy, and discarnate spirits can manipulate that energy in many ways to achieve their goals. Not all spirits are nice, and some enjoy manipulating those on the earth plane for revenge for a life that has been cut short, or because their life wasn't what they wanted. Sometimes they play with people's thoughts and feelings just because they can.

Religion is manmade and can be a beautiful thing all the while people are not manipulated. It is the rituals and interpretation of the religious writings that often destroy the purpose of faith.

Some spirits are atheists who don't believe in religion or that life continues after death. Imagine what it would feel like if you suddenly found you had died but were still aware of yourself and still had thoughts and feelings. There are also spirits who know they have passed over but have been told they will be met by Jesus, or God and will wait until they come for them. I have spoken to many nuns who have passed, who think because they have not been met, they have failed in some way and thought they would have to do penance before entering heaven. It's not that surprising when you consider a lifetime of being told what to expect. There are also many people who expect to go to heaven, but because of the way they died, either can't find heaven or think they're in hell, because where they are it's always dark and cold.

The departed spirits' consciousness is locked on to the physical world because that's what they're used to. They still see with their physical eyes and so are not aware of the changes that have occurred in passing to spirit. They will not see the spirit world or the spirits around them because the spirit world doesn't have eyes; they use their senses to see. Many mediums don't see spirit but sense them. What they sense is as clear as seeing someone with the added benefit of feeling emotions as well. Many don't hear either but receive thoughts or impressions, which is the way spirit communicate with us and each other. So, it's no wonder the newly departed can easily be confused and disorientated. When you don't have this knowledge, but get feelings, pains, and thoughts or voices while still on the earth plane, it can and does cause confusion and in many cases great distress. People don't always like to be different when they don't know why or what's happening to them. By having a greater understanding of the reality of life, where we come from and where we go when we die. This understanding that should be natural would negate hauntings, and the confusion people can have when they pass from the physical world back to their natural state of being.

All over the world in all cultures, there is the belief in spirits in one way or another. Each religion has its good and evil spirits who it's believed will help or hinder according to the rites or rituals being performed. Each religion has a name for each of its

Angels & Demons, and they will be called upon as required. Religion is manmade therefore the *Angels & Demons* must also be manmade. So, calling on a certain angel or demon wouldn't have any effect on the outcome of an exorcism or spirit removal, whether it be archangels, gods, or demons. It is the intent behind what is being done, and the spiritual connections the practitioner has that makes it work. A prayer or religious text being recited will have no effect if the discarnate spirit doesn't have the same beliefs as the person carrying out the removal or rescue. In all the years and the many houses, I've visited, I have never used a particular faith or rite to remove spirits. I have found that by talking to them and treating them as intelligent beings, I have been able to help them to move on, sometimes after people from religious organisations, have been and had no success. There are spirits who are being nasty are not stupid, and know far more about the realities of religion and life than we do. Where the spirit is lost, or confused, just by explaining what has happened to them and showing them the way to heaven has saved a lot of people and spirits years of torment. Although there is no time in spirit, it doesn't change the torture some go through while trying to find help.

There are many beliefs about how to remove spirits more than I can list, but a few of the more common ones are smudging with smouldering sage. It makes the area being smudged smell fresh and clean but has no effect on any spirits that are around, as they are energy and sage whether burnt or not is physical. Likewise, with salt and holy water, although used because they are said to be pure or blessed, they won't have any effect if the spirit doesn't believe. Prayers, rituals, Icons and religious text also don't have any effect if the spirit is not of the same inclination. It can take so long as two years of repeated visits by the exorcist to remove an invading spirit in a Christian exorcism, and I suspect the spirit finally goes because there's too much interference. They prefer an easy life too and if things get too much like hard work they'll move on. But where do they move on to? Someone else who they can bother without interference. That's why it's better to treat spirit as individual intelligent beings and deal with them according to their needs.

Here are a few cases we have dealt with; however, the names and locations have been changed to protect the people involved. There are some we can help and some we can't, and those on medication for mental illness often have interference as well. Although we are aware we will not remove them permanently, we know we're able to calm things down for a while.

A Haunting in Hampshire

It was towards the end of October 2011 that our team received a call from a lady named Tina. Tina asked if we could help, as she had paranormal activity in her house. She said it started just after Christmas 2010 when her daughter, Alice, and her granddaughter, Joyce, were staying with them. Joyce had received a toy cooker for Christmas, which played a tune as the timer ran down. Late one evening just after everyone had gone to bed the music started to play and then stopped. No one took any notice because they thought it was just the spring winding down. But it played again in the middle of the night, so Tina's husband, Harry, went downstairs and took the batteries out. It was then he realised the tune was played by battery, not springs.

Harry returned upstairs but no sooner had he got into bed than the music played again. Harry awakened Tina and told her what had happened, but she just thought he was dreaming. While they were talking, much to Tina's surprise, the tune played again. Tina and Harry went downstairs and when Harry showed Tina the space where the batteries went, Tina went a little pale. They couldn't understand how it had played, so they decided to deal with it in the morning. They returned to bed to get a good night's sleep. Alas, it was not to be, because after they had been in bed for about ten minutes, the tune played again. After about an hour of repeated playing, it suddenly stopped, and they dozed off. The following morning, they decided to take the toy back and get a replacement.

Over the next few nights, Alice complained that it was freezing in the room where she was sleeping. Harry checked the radiator and said it was working fine, but he couldn't explain why it was so cold in there. That night Joyce woke up crying and would not stay in the room where she was sleeping. She said there were strange people in the room. When Alice took her back to her room, she told Tina there was an eerie feeling in the room her daughter was sleeping in, and she felt it would be better for all of them if she had her daughter in with her.

The next day after Alice and Joyce had gone home, Tina and Harry were left to wonder what was going on. Over the next few months, they heard strange noises and bangs but tried to ignore them. Each time Joyce came to stay the bedroom she was sleeping in got icy, and she seemed to get very agitated. In fact, Alice complained she was like it every time she came home after staying with her grandparents, and it took a few days for her to calm down again.

One day Tina went into the downstairs toilet only to find she was standing in a pool of water. She thought there was a leak and after mopping it up asked Harry to check and see if he could find the problem. Upon investigation by her husband and a plumber friend, no water leaks could be found, and no explanation could be given for how the water got there. There were only Tina and Harry in the house at the time. Tina also said on another occasion about a month later she was cooking Sunday lunch. When she opened a kitchen cupboard, the salt and pepper pots were thrown at her, narrowly missing her head. When Tina shouted in surprise, Harry rushed in to see what the commotion was about, but there was nothing to see except the salt and pepper pots on the floor. When I asked how Tina had found us, she said a friend at the local spiritualist church had told her about us. She asked if we would be able to help her. I replied yes, we would come around and deal with it for her. I told her there would be three of our team coming if that was OK. Tina said that would be great.

Upon arrival, a few days later I introduced our team to Tina and Harry. There was Jane, Danny and myself. The first thing we noticed was a deep foreboding atmosphere pervading the whole house. We sat down and discussed the problems that Tina and Harry were experiencing. It so happened, that Joyce was staying with them when we visited. Because Joyce was so young, Harry said he would take her out and would Tina call him when we'd finished.

I explained that an energy field, a sort of protection, had been created around their house by our guides, so the spirits couldn't leave until we had talked to them. Once we had ascertained whether they wanted to go to heaven or not, we could help where needed. When we had finished, there would be no spirits left inside the protection. Although occasionally their loved ones could come and visit, they would not let their presence be known. I explained to Tina that one of us would go into a light trance and bring the spirits through to talk so that she could hear what they had to say. I asked if there were any questions before we started and Tina asked how many we had found around her house. I explained there was more than one and they were scattered around the house.

There were two upstairs in the back bedroom and quite a few in the small bedroom at the front of the house. She said the small bedroom was always cold, and when Joyce came, she was afraid to sleep in that room. I told her there were no evil spirits in the main bedroom but there were some on the stairs watching us. There was a little boy in the downstairs toilet with polio and a number of what could only be described as urchins in the lounge with a stern looking woman. In the dining room, there was a nasty looking man who was dressed as a vicar, with a dog collar, who had a cane in his hand, and there were some children in the kitchen. After everyone had settled down, I asked Jane to bring through a nasty looking man who was standing by the stairs. This is how the conversation went:

"Good afternoon," I said.

"What do you want here?" the man asked.

"I want to know why you're here and what you're doing," I replied.

He said, "That's none of your business. I don't want to talk to you, and you should leave before you get yourselves in trouble."

"We're not leaving; we're here to sort out the problems that you and your friends are causing, to the people that live in the house."

"What happens in this house is no business of yours, it's our house, and we'll do what we like."

"It is our business Tina and Harry asked us to sort it out, which gives us the authority to question and remove those of you that are causing trouble."

"Well there's nothing you can do so get out. I no longer want to talk to you, and if you know what's good for you, you'll leave."

It was obvious we weren't going to get much if any information from him so I decided to remove him and his associates and move on. I said. "We won't leave until we have done what we came here for; if you would like to go to heaven we would be happy to help you. We're staying until we have finished the job we came to do. The alternative is for us to escort you off the premises, where you'll find yourself in the hands of our guides who will help you to understand your situation."

"Well, I don't want to go to heaven, and my friends and I are staying here."

"I'm sorry but there are only two choices and staying here is not one of them; if you don't leave, we'll have to remove you," I said.

He refused to leave so we had to escort him and his friends out. Once we had watched them go, Jane opened her eyes as she came out of trance. As they left our guides placed an energy field around them and took them to a place where they couldn't upset anyone else while they talked to them.

Tina asked: "What if they came back?"

I explained about the energy field that was put around the spirits. It would make it difficult for them to carry on with what they were doing, and that the protection would stop them from coming back.

She asked: "Why couldn't you stop them permanently?"

"They have free will, and we are not able nor would we wish to take that away from anyone. They'll come to an understanding eventually, but obviously, that time is not now."

I asked Danny to get the vicar who was in the dining room, and we would see what he had to say. When the vicar came through it got icy, but we ignored that and just carried on.

I asked: "Good afternoon, vicar, how can we help you?"

"You can stop meddling in things you don't know anything about and leave while you're still sane," he replied.

"May I ask why you're here?"

"I'm here to make sure the children behave and learn the word of God."

"How do you make them behave?"

"Children have to learn when to speak and when to be silent."

"Is that why you have the cane to show them who is the boss?"

"I do God's work, and if it means I have to beat the Devil out of them, then they should thank me for putting them on the road to salvation."

"Is that why the children are here?"

"They're wayward and they've been put here so we can straighten them out; they will then grow up as God-fearing adults."

"So, this is a home, and you are in charge of their education is, that, right?"

"Enough of this be on your way and don't interfere."

"I'm sorry, but you don't seem to realise you have passed over and so have the children, you should be with your God now and so should they. You should all be at peace, and the children are no longer your responsibility."

"Don't be ridiculous, whether I'm alive or not doesn't matter. Don't you realise it's their last chance before the Devil gets them? I cannot let him win; these children must learn to respect their elders and behave."

"I'm afraid we're going to have to take them to heaven; we'll take you too if you want to go."

"How dare you! Who do you think you are? Meddling in things beyond your comprehension will get you into a lot of trouble, my boy?"

"Am I to take it that you don't want us to take you to heaven?"

"I no longer wish to talk to you… you're in the Devil's hands, and if you don't stop what you're doing, you will never be saved."

"OK then as you don't want our help we'll have to send you away from here. If at any time, you come to your senses, then just ask out loud for help, and someone will be there for you. Now I'm afraid you must leave, our guides are here to escort you to a place where you will find peace. Goodbye."

"I will return and make you learn the lessons of the bible you'll see," he said as he left.

We thought it would be best to sort the children out, so I explained to Tina it was better if I could get them to realise they were dead rather than tell them, as it sometimes came as quite a shock to them.

I asked Danny to bring through one of the children who was in the kitchen. The little girl he brought through was about ten years old and looked as though she hadn't eaten in weeks. She was dirty, and her clothes were not much better than rags. I asked her what her name was.

"My name is Grace, sir," she said.

"Hello, Grace. I'm Mike. Are you alright?" I asked.

"Yes, I suppose so, but that man was horrible, he was always hitting us for no reason."

"Well, he's gone now. Can you tell me what happened to you? What's the last thing you remember?"

"Well we were all in the big room asleep, and it got very dark and smelled horrible, my eyes started hurting, and I couldn't breathe."

"Why do you think that was?"

"I don't know it got hot, then I went to sleep again."

"What happened next?"

"I was standing up; it was very dark. But I could see a little girl on the floor. I don't know who she was, but she looked unhappy, even though she was asleep."

"Was that little girl about your age and looked a bit like you?"

"Yes, she did, was it me?"

"If it was you what do you think must have happened to you?"

"If I was looking down at me, I can't be standing up and lying down. Does that mean I died?"

"Yes, it does. Where do people go when they die?"

"If you're good you go to God, and if you're bad, you go to the Devil. The vicar said we were all bad and we would go to hell. Is that where we are?"

"No, you're lost, and we've come to take you to heaven. Would you and your friends like to go there?"

"Will we be allowed? The vicar said we would never go to heaven because we were bad."

"You're not bad, and yes you can go to heaven. Would you all like to go?"

"Yes please, can we all go together, please?" Grace was quite excited.

"Yes of course, then you'll have your friends with you in heaven, won't you. Was it one of the children who threw the salt and pepper pots at the lady?"

"Yes, only we were throwing them at the matron because she was pulling my friend's hair. I'm sorry if it frightened her, we didn't mean to."

"That's alright, at least you got yourselves noticed, that's one of the reasons we're here now. It was one of your friends making the music play as well wasn't it?"

"Yes, she liked to listen to it, it made her happy."

"OK that's alright, now can you open your eyes big and wide and tell me what you can see?" The reason we ask the spirits to open their eyes is that we want them to open their senses to see, which is how the spirit world see things. That's one of the reasons people get lost; they are only aware of the earth plane.

"I can see a long tunnel with a light at the end."

"OK, that's the light from heaven you can see; when you're ready we're going to take you there. Are you or your friends in any pain?"

"Yes, and one of the boys has got a shrivelled leg, so don't go too fast, because he won't be able to keep up and he might get lost," she said with concern. Since they are spirit and not physical, their physical ailments no longer exist in the spirit world, but because they have been aware in life of their ailments they don't even consider their spirit cannot be less than the whole. Therefore, when we remove their pain and discomfort, what we're doing is asking our guides to help the spirits realise they no longer need to carry their illness or disfigurements.

"Well let's make everyone better first, we're going to take the pain away and make your friends leg better; everyone alright now?"

"Oh, thank you, he can walk now, and he's jumping up and down."

"OK, now we can go to heaven."

When we arrived in heaven the children knew no one, they had been abandoned as babies so we asked our guides to find someone to look after them. They brought forward some kind ladies who took the children away to safety. We then spoke to the matron, and after we had explained what had happened to her, she asked us if she could go to heaven. We said we would take her to meet her husband. She told us the children were in a home for wayward children, and there had been a fire, and all had perished.

We then brought the little boy with polio through.

"Hello, what's your name?"

"My name's Colin, who are you?"

"We've come to help you; do you know what's happened to you?"

"I was in a hospital, and I was very ill, it went dark, and then I was here. Do you know where my mummy is, I can't find her, she was with me in hospital, but now she's gone."

"What happens to people when they're very ill?"

"Sometimes they die, and sometimes they get better."

"Do you think you got better?"

"No, I'd still be with mummy if I was, so I must have died."

"Yes, I'm afraid so, but that was a long time ago, you've been lost for a while, and then you were brought here."

"I'm sorry about the water. I tried to wash and couldn't turn the water off."

"That's OK, no harm done."

"Why can't I be with mummy?"

"You can, now that you understand what's happened to you. First, we're going to make you better, and then we're going to take you to your mummy. How do you feel now?"

"I feel much better and my arms and hands are alright now. Where's my mummy, I want to show her," he said excitedly.

"Open your eyes and tell me what you can see."

"I can see a big light just over there."

"OK, we're going into that light, it's the entrance to heaven."

"Will mummy be there? She wasn't old you know."

"I know, but that was a long time ago... she grew old and died, and she's waiting for you. Can you see her over there?"

"Oh yes, can I go to her, please?"

"Yes, off you go."

"Thank you."

"You're welcome," I said as he went running over to his mother and the rest of his family.

We spoke to the remainder of the lost souls who were in the house and resolved their problems; once it was clear, the atmosphere seemed to lighten. Tina telephoned us a week later as we had asked her to; she said things were peaceful and quiet now. She said Joyce was OK now and she was quite happy to sleep in the front bedroom again.

When she went home, she was her usual self, so her mother was less concerned about her staying with her grandparents. We should remember the pains and ailments of the body, only belong to the physical, and the spirit body is always whole. The reason the spirits suffer is that they don't realise they no longer have a physical body to feel pain. That's why we can make them feel better. We spent three hours at Tina's house and by talking directly to the spirits we could resolve the situation for all concerned.

Conclusion

In this case, there wasn't any apparent reason for the family's problems that we were aware of. There may have been an underlying reason for their heightened awareness; it could have been Joyce being a bit sensitive. We will never know for sure but I suspect it's a bit of Joyce's sensitivity and Alice and her parents heightened awareness for Joyce.

The names have been changed to provide anonymity as this visit only took place on October 28th, 2011.

A Haunting in Brighton, West Sussex

I was asked to go to a house near Brighton because the lady whose name was Jane was having spiritual problems. I asked her what problems she was getting and Jane said, "There are spirits in my house doing all sorts of things that are frightening me. I moved in about six months ago, and things have got steadily worse."

"What kind of things?" I asked.

"Most nights my bed is being shaken, sometimes somebody gets into bed with me. One night as I got out of bed someone grabbed my ankle, and I had to kick to get them off. When I turned the light on there was no one there. I hear loud bangs coming from the bedroom at the front of the house, day and night. Lights turn on and off by themselves. I live alone, and I'm frightened. Can you do anything to stop it?"

"I'll bring one of my colleagues, and we'll remove the spirits that are causing you so many problems."

When we arrived, we both felt an evil presence, and as I walked through the house, I was aware of quite a few spirits, good and bad. Jane told us the house had been empty for a while before she moved in. We sat down, and I explained how we were going to remove the spirits and asked if she had any questions before we started.

"How many are there?" Jane asked.

"There's quite a few," I said, "but we'll deal with them." I explained to her that my colleague Danny would go into a light trance and bring the spirits through so all could hear what was said.

"What's light trance?" Jane asked.

"It's when a medium allows a spirit to overshadow them and use their voice to speak with us. They will be controlled by the medium in so far as they can only stay as long as the medium allows them to. Danny will draw the spirits to him, and they won't be able to leave until he lets them, as Danny will only be in a light trance he will be aware of what's going on at all times, and can come out of trance just by opening her eyes. There's nothing to be afraid of it's just as though Danny has closed his eyes."

She seemed satisfied for the moment, and we decided to proceed with the removal of the spirits. We started with the man who was messing around in the bedroom, and I asked Danny to bring him through. I asked him his name that he refused to give saying it was none of my business. So, I asked him why he was frightening the lady by shaking her bed and grabbing her leg.

"I'm looking after her," he said.

"How're you doing that?" I replied.

"By letting her know, she isn't alone and there's someone around."

"There are nicer ways of doing that; she doesn't want your help, and she wants you to leave."

"I'm quite comfortable in the house and wasn't planning on leaving for some time."

"Do you know where you are apart from being in the house?"

"I'm just in this house, and it's better than the dark and cold where I have been."

"Do you know what's happened to you?"

"The last thing I remember is falling down the stairs. I was unconscious, and they took me to the hospital."

"How do you know you were taken to the hospital if you were unconscious?"

He thought for a moment. "Because I saw them take me." Then he said, "I could see myself lying at the bottom of the stairs and thought how's this happening. They took me to the ambulance and drove off. Then I was somewhere else, and it was cold and dark. I saw this house with a light above it and came in; I don't want to go out there again, so I'm going to stay here."

I asked him: "How could you be in two places at once, looking at yourself at the bottom of the stairs and lying on the floor?"

That made him think, and then he realised he couldn't, and that's when he realised he was dead because he said, "I must be dead then."

"Yes, you are, and it's not nice to frighten people; where do you think people go when they die?"

"They will go to heaven or hell depending on how good they've been."

"Would you like to go to heaven?"

"I don't think they would let me go there because I haven't been very nice to the lady that lives here."

"You can go to heaven, and I'm sure the Jane wouldn't object. What's your name?"

"Albert," he replied.

"So, Mary is your wife then?" I said.

That took him a little by surprise, and he asked, "How do you know?"

"As I tune into you I'm able to pick up on your wife who's in heaven; would you like to see her again?"

"If I'm allowed, yes I would."

"We'll take you to her." We took him to the light, where she was waiting.

As they hugged, they both said, "Thank you."

Before we said goodbye, I asked him one last question: "What year did you have your accident?"

"1907."

When Danny opened his eyes, Jane was in tears as she had felt the emotions of their reunion.

When she settled down, I said, "We have a few more to talk to is that OK?"

"Yes, I hope they're not all as lost as he was."

I asked Danny to bring through the woman who was standing in the corner watching us. When she came through, I asked: "How can we help you?"

"I have a lot of lost children here that I've been looking after; can you take us to heaven, please?"

"Of course we will. Are they all aware of what's happened to them?"

"I've told them they've died, and that I'm trying to find a way of taking them to see their families. That's why they stayed with me."

We gathered all the children together and took them and the lady to heaven where they met with their families. I thought it was time to deal with the man I had picked up in the spare bedroom, where we'd been hearing noises ever since we arrived.

"There's a man of average build with not much hair," I said. "He isn't a particularly happy man, and he's throwing his weight around, and that's why we're hearing noises." Danny closed his eyes and brought the man through.

"What do you think you're doing?" he said. "I've just sorted out who I want in my house, and you come along and start taking them away."

I pointed out that it wasn't his house and those we had spoken to had gone to a better place, where their loved ones were.

He was angry: "How dare you interfere with my plans; this is my house, I claimed it, and I will do what I like in my own home."

I asked him if he knew what had happened to him and he said, "Yes of course." I asked him to tell me, and he replied, "I died in a fire, and I've been wandering all over till I found this house."

"You can't stay here; this house belongs to the lady, and she wants to be left in peace."

"There's plenty of room. Why does she have to be so greedy? Once I've rearranged a few things I'm sure we can get along"

I told him he didn't belong and the lady wanted him out, I asked him: "Where should people go when they die?"

"Wherever they can find some peace."

"There are other places where you can go, where you wouldn't upset the living."

"Oh, do you mean heaven?"

"Yes, if you want to."

"It's not real, I haven't seen it, and I've looked."

"It is real, but you aren't looking in the right way."

"What do you mean in the right way? I can see you."

"But you don't live in this world anymore, and you can't see everything in your world. Let me show you what you're missing."

"OK, how will you do that?"

"Simple, open your eyes, and you'll see a lot of people you've been missing."

"Where did they come from?"

"They've been there all along; now you're looking with your senses instead of your eyes and you're now looking in your world."

"But I still can't see heaven," he said.

"That's because you don't know where to look; what else can you see apart from those strange people?"

"I can see a tunnel with a light at the end."

"Yes, that's the entrance to heaven. Shall we go and see your family?"

"They won't be there, yet I'm only 35, they were all too young to die when I did."

"What year did you die?" I asked.

"1933," he said.

When I told him it was 2011, he was very surprised as he hadn't been aware of that much time passing.

"Are you ready for me to take you to see them?" I asked.

"Well if they'll have me in heaven, I haven't been all that nice you know."

"Yes, I know, but you can still go to heaven; there are people there who've done far worse than you."

"OK, let's go and see." So, I took him to meet his family and to his surprise they were all there waiting for him. He said thanks and asked if he could stay.

"Of course," I said, "go in peace." And then he left.

When Danny opened his eyes, he said, "There were a lot of people, family and friends waiting for him, and he got all choked up."

Jane asked if there were any more.

"Yes," I said. "We've got a young boy standing over there who looks like he could do with some help. He's about 12 years old with dark hair and nothing on his feet, and he's dressed in dirty grey trousers, which come down to his knees and has a grey top on."

"Yes," said Danny. "I can sense him. Do you want me to bring him through?"

Yes, please," I said. When the boy was through I asked his name.

"Tom," he said.

"Do you know where you are?" I asked.

"No, I've been wandering in the dark, and it was cold until I saw this house and came in. It's warm here, but there were some nasty people here, so I had to hide."

"What's the last thing you remember before you were in the dark?"

"I was working up a chimney, and I got stuck and they couldn't get me out."

"I see, then what happened?"

"I was there for a long time, and my nose got blocked with soot. I tried to open my mouth to breathe, but it got filled with soot. My chest hurt and that's all I can remember."

"So, what do you think happens when you can't breathe?"

"You die; is that what happened to me?"

"Yes, I'm afraid it is."

"But if I'm dead, how can I talk to you?"

"Well, your body's dead but the real you is still alive in another way."

"Do you mean I'm a ghost?"

"That's sometimes what they call you, but I prefer to call you a spirit. Are you in any pain?"

"Well my chest is hurting, and my sides are sore."

"We'll take that away so you'll feel better... there, how's that?"

With a smile, Tom said, "Yes and I can breathe again; what do I do now?"

"Would you like to go to heaven?"

"Is that where dead people go?"

"Yes, it's where you came from before you were born; where your mum and dad and all your family are."

"But they can't be; they were all right when I went to work."

"What year was it when you died?"

"I don't know, 1800 and something, I think."

"Well, it's 2011 now, that's more than two hundred years ago, you've been dead a long time. Would you like us to take you to heaven so you can see them again?"

"Yes please, I don't want to stay here."

"OK, open your eyes and tell me what you can see."

"I can see a big light."

"Yes, that's the entrance to heaven; we're going to go into that tunnel to heaven, but before we go can you see the other children in this house?" I asked.

"Yes, there are quite a few; can they come with us?"

"Yes, our guides are just getting them lined up. OK, now we're ready to go, it won't take long."

"What're guides?" Tom asked.

"They're friends of ours who help us to help people like you when you're lost. They work with us from your side of life. Here we are, what can you see now?"

"I can see lots of people, and there's me mum and dad, can I go now?"

"Yes, you're safe now, goodbye."

"Goodbye and thanks, mister." All the children went to their loved ones, and Danny opened his eyes.

Jane said: "There were a lot of people here, is that all of them?"

"Yes, now you can have a bit of peace and quiet."

"Will they come back again?" Jane asked.

"No, they won't, we've put protection around your house so you won't get others coming to disturb you. What you need to do now is get on with your life. Don't think about whether there's anyone here. That would be an invitation for others to come through the protection."

"What's protection and how does it work?" Jane asked.

"It's an energy field that our guides put up before we come, so the nasty ones can't run away and come back after we've been. Then when we've finished, they show your guides how to keep it there so that you won't be bothered again."

We chatted a bit then said our goodbyes to Jane, knowing she wouldn't have any more problems. I telephoned Jane a few weeks later just to make sure she was alright, and she said since we had been to her house she'd had no more problems. Jane doesn't get aches or pains like before and she's sleeping much better now.

Conclusion

In this case, the house already had spirits; this often occurs in empty houses because the spirits want somewhere to go where they can assess their new situation. When Jane moved in, they realised she was aware of them and they accepted her as part of their community. By interacting with her they frightened her, which is understandable since to them she was real, yet to her, they were noises and feelings she didn't understand. There's nothing more frightening than hearing and feeling things when there's no one there.

A Haunting in Gosport Hampshire

We were asked to visit a lady named Caroline whose eldest daughter was being attacked by unseen entities as she put it. When we arrived, the atmosphere was very dense, and the eldest daughter was very depressed. It was not surprising as everything seemed to be going against her. She had money problems, no job and her relationship had fallen apart.

Caroline was in her early forties with a daughter of nineteen named Sheila, a son of fourteen, and daughter of three. The atmosphere in the house was very negative, and I was aware of some malevolent spirits around the home.

She wasn't sleeping too well, not surprising really, and her daughter was not in a good place, what with all that had been going on.

After introductions, I asked Caroline to bring us up to date on what had been going on. She told us that Sheila had seen the faces of spirits on her bedroom wall, even in the dark, and her duvet was being dragged off her bed when she was trying to sleep. She was also being poked and prodded when she was asleep, so was repeatedly being woken up.

Because she was so tired, she had lost her job, and Sheila was getting more and more depressed.

I asked when all this started and was it affecting anyone else. Caroline said it had started about two months ago, and no one else seemed to be affected except herself. Caroline was seeing shapes and hearing noises but hadn't said anything because she didn't want to frighten the children.

I asked if anyone had been doing anything to try to communicate with the spirit world, as I had a feeling someone had been dabbling with a Ouija board. Sheila said she and her friends had been using a Ouija board to try to talk to a spirit. I explained how dangerous this was as when using the Ouija board, it was the same as ringing a number at random on the telephone. Most of the time you get reasonable people, but sometimes you will get a nasty person. With the Ouija board once you invite a spirit to come and communicate they don't always leave. Once they realise they can talk with people on the physical plane, they find they enjoy it, especially when the see that you can't stop them. They don't need sleep so they can and do pester you at all hours. Because they think they have been invited, they can be difficult to remove unless you're strong willed. They'll also prey on your insecurities and often stay with you and can cause pains, depression and mood changes as well as show themselves and move things.

I asked if there were any questions and Sheila asked, "Will you be able to remove them?"

"Yes," I said. "Providing you listen and do what we tell you, then you'll have no more problems."

I told Caroline and her family that Danny would close his eyes and go into a light trance. While Danny was in a trance, he would be able to bring the spirits through so she could hear what they had to say.

"Please don't say anything unless I ask you to while Danny has his eyes closed. I will be tuning into the spirit I'm talking to and watching you all, to make sure you don't get attacked while we're working," I said.

"Why would they attack us?" Caroline asked.

"To distract us from what we're doing. They don't always bother you while we're here; I just wanted to warn you. Don't worry, everything will be alright."

I asked Danny to start by bringing a man through who was standing by the door watching us.

Danny closed his eyes and as he sensed the man Danny drew him in and brought him through.

"Hello, how are you?" I asked.

"I'm well thank you, not that it's any of your business. What do you want?"

"I thought we'd have a chat and see if we could help each other. How did you get here?" I asked.

"I came with her; she invited me." He pointed in Sheila's direction.

"What's your name?"

"It's Frederic and yours?"

"I'm Mike, do you know what's happened to you?"

"I was minding my own business when she called me, said is anybody there. I was a bit confused with what had happened and when I heard her I thought she might know. It turns out she didn't even know what she was doing, and now I'm stuck with her."

"Why are you stuck with her?"

"Every time I try to leave I get drawn back; it doesn't matter what I do, I can't go."

"We can help you with that; where are you trying to go?"

"Anywhere except here. There are some nasty people around her, and I don't want to get involved with them."

"What're they doing?"

"They're playing all sorts of games; they poke her and whisper in her ear and move things. I think they're trying to scare her and, judging by how she reacts, they're succeeding."

"Alright, Frederic, let's get you out of here. Do you know what's happened to you?"

"Yes, I died, but I wasn't expecting this. I thought when you were dead that was it."

"How did you die?"

"I had a massive pain in my head, and that was it. I still can't get rid of the pain."

"You know the pain is a memory. It belongs to your body; it can't affect your spirit unless you let it. We'll ask our guides to take the pain away for you, is that better?"

"Yes, it's starting to go now, thanks. Can you take me away from here?"

"Yes, do you know about heaven?"

"I've heard the usual stuff; is it true is there a place like that?"

"Yes, do you want us to take you there?"

"Yes please, as I understand it my family are there?"

"That's right. Open your eyes and tell me what you can see," I said.

"I can see a lot of people, but they look different. Where did they come from?"

"They are spirit people; many are our guides who help us, and there are some who're also lost like you. Can you see anything else?"

"It's like I'm looking at the glow of light behind them... it's quite bright you know."

"That's the light from heaven where we're going to take you. We'll also take some of the other lost spirits as well. Let's get everyone together, and we'll get going?"

"Yes, that would be fine, there are a lot of people who want to go; can you take them all?"

"We'll take all those who want to go. Is your wife's name Margaret?"

"Yes, she's not there, is she?"

"Yes, she passed about fifteen years after you."

"How can that be; I've only just got here myself."

"What year did you die?"

"It would be about 1947. What year is it now?"

It's 2015 now, so you have been in limbo for nearly seventy years."

"It feels like it was yesterday."

"Yes, there's no time in the spirit realms; shall we take you to heaven then?"

"Yes please."

I walked with him and all the others into the light where his wife and son were waiting. As he joined his family, I saw many other people come forward to greet him. There were a lot of family reunions as the other lost souls found their families. I had to return to the room as the emotions were getting quite strong and I knew I had others to deal with who wouldn't be so nice.

As Danny opened his eyes, he said, "It was like walking into a massive room full of people waiting for them, only it wasn't a room. The light was like the sun was coming up, but there was no sun, just a big yellow glow behind them as we came forward, beautiful." Caroline asked if they had all gone and I explained: "There are more to deal with; that was just the beginning. There are still the spirits that have been annoying Sheila and making noises to sort out. Danny, can you see that lady with the overcoat, she is about sixty with curly grey hair, about five foot two."

"Yes, you mean the woman over by the chair?"

"Yes, can you bring her through please?"

"OK."

When the lady came through you could see by the expression on Danny's face she wasn't happy.

"Hello, how are you? You don't look too happy to see us," I said.

"Happy, why would I be happy? I don't like interfering people poking their noses into my business. What do you want?"

"We would just like to talk about why you're here and see if we can help," I said.

"I don't wish to speak to you, and I don't need any help. I'm doing just fine."

"Ah, but what are you doing, not trying to upset these nice people are you?"

"I'm just doing what I like to do; if it upsets them, then they know what they can do, leave."

"Why should they leave? This is their house, and you don't belong here, so you should leave."

It was at that point that Sheila said she was suddenly feeling sick.

"You can tell your friends to leave her alone; it's not necessary, and it won't stop us. If they don't stop you will force us to take steps to quarantine your associates."

"Do your worst; you won't get rid of me so easily."

I asked my guides to restrain her associates and restrict her ability to affect anyone in the room.

"You have forced me to control your friends; as you can see, they aren't very happy with you for getting them into this mess. Now behave yourself and let's talk about how we can resolve this situation."

"You're good; I wasn't expecting that. The last time I met someone like you, they couldn't leave fast enough."

"We'll see. We work as a team; our guides on your side of life, and us on this side. What were the last people doing that you scared them so easily?"

"They were saying prayers and sprinkling holy water around and saying 'demon get out'. We just watched until we got fed up and then scared them off. Do I look like a demon?"

"It can be deceiving, but you look like someone's granny to me who's having a bad time. Why are you trying to frighten these people?"

"I'm having the time of my life, and I'm just playing with them. You should see what I can do if I'm annoyed."

"I'm sure you can do other things, but you won't do them here. Why don't you go to heaven and be with your family and leave these people to live their lives in peace? Don't you think they've got enough problems without you adding to them?"

"Are you saying I'm a problem for them? If it weren't me, it would be someone else. You can't get rid of all of us."

"Well we can, but you now have your own problems. Do you think your friends will thank you for getting them into trouble?"

"Ha, they won't do anything, they're afraid of me. I might look like a granny, but I'm good at what I do."

"So are we and it's time for you to leave. You can go to heaven, or we'll be forced to put you in limbo until you see the error of your ways. We would like to take you to heaven where you can find some peace. I know you're hurting inside because of what was done to you, but there's no need to take it out on this family, they didn't do anything to you."

"You have no idea how I feel. You weren't there and why would I go to heaven; he'll probably be there, and I don't want to see him ever."

"I do have an idea. You don't have to see him if you don't want to. Heaven is a big place you know, and there are a lot of friends waiting for you."

"I thought we had to stay together forever; that's what we promised. Do you mean I can see my children and never have to see him?"

"Yes, you can be with your children and grandchildren; you can also be with all of your family and friends. It's just him who won't be there."

"Can I have a look first just to make sure you're not just trying to get me out?"

"Yes, you can have a look; if you open your eyes, you'll see all of your family waiting for you. They know you're there but can't see you. If you want to be with them, I'll have to take you. As far as getting you out we could have done that without talking to you, but we wanted to help you."

"I can see them; I didn't realise how many of them were dead, it must be a long time since I was killed. What year is it now?"

"It's 2015, so you've been in the spirit realms for about 120 years haven't you. Do you want us to take you to heaven?"

"I didn't think it was that long. Yes, I would like to be with my family. What're you going to do with this lot?"

"Those who want to go to heaven can come with us; those who don't want to go will be removed from here and put in a place where their guides can talk to them. They can't leave or come back here and eventually they'll go to heaven."

"There's a lot of them that want to go to heaven, can we go?"

"Let's get everyone together, and I'll take you."

"We're ready. Sorry about upsetting these people, I was in a bad place."

"We all make mistakes. Shall we go into the light?"

"The light is warm; it's been a long time since I've felt the warmth and peace. You don't realise what you're missing until you get it back. I can see them now; can I go, please."

"Yes, go in peace."

"Thank you, you are good people."

Danny opened his eyes and said, "I thought she was going to be awkward and be troublesome."

"I thought if I just chatted with her it would be easier for all concerned. When you get into a conversation with some of these people, they forget to attack you, and it's easier to sort them out."

"Yes, she seemed to calm down when she was talking."

Sheila asked: "What about the ones who didn't go to heaven, are they still here?"

"No," I said. "They were taken away by our guides to a place where they will to stay until they reform their ways."

"How do you know they all went?"

Danny said, "I see them being collected and taken away by our guides while we're taking the others to heaven."

"So those were the ones that were poking me and pulling my duvet?" Sheila asked.

"Yes, but there are others here who have been talking to you and making you feel that you were being watched. We're going to deal with them now," I said.

"Oh, OK," Sheila said.

I asked Danny to bring the man who was standing behind Caroline through so we could see why he was there.

As the man came through he seemed very calm and controlled.

"Hello, what's your name?" I asked.

"It's Joseph," he replied. "How can I help you?"

"By telling us why you're here and what you've being doing," I said.

"I'm here because I like it here and as to what I've been doing, that's my business."

"What do you hope to achieve by whispering in Sheila's ear all the time and staring at her," I said.

"Well that would seem fairly obvious; she was starting to think she was a bit loony because we talk to her, and nobody else could hear us."

"That's blown that then because she knows now that you're real and what you've been doing. Not much left for you to do now except leave is there."

"Oh, there's plenty more we can do; it won't take long to get her back to where she was before you turned up. She thinks she's a medium and asks all sorts of questions about her friends."

I turned to Sheila and said, "If you want to develop your mediumship you should go to a development circle. The first thing they should teach you is how to shut down, so you're not bothered by spirits when you're not tuning in. It may seem like a way of finding out what your friends have been up to, but that's not what it's about. It's about helping people who have lost someone when they die. To prove survival and take away the fear of death, it's not for fun or personal gain."

"I just asked about little things, and they told me."

"Yes I know, it's easy to get drawn in, but we have to respect other people's privacy. Otherwise, people would be afraid you might give away their secrets. That's why it's important to go to a development circle; they will teach you what is acceptable to say. One of my rules is never to say something that might embarrass anyone. We'll talk about that after we've sorted this lot out."

"OK, I'm sorry. I didn't know."

"That's alright; we all have to start somewhere. Now, Joseph, why don't you leave these people alone and take your friends to heaven where you can all be with your families?"

"Why should we? We're quite happy here… we've got everything we want."

"You should leave because what you're doing is interfering with their lives. How would you like it if when you were on the earth plane, you had someone talking to you and making you feel paranoid?"

"We like it here so we're staying."

"I'm sorry we can't let you stay here; you can go to heaven, or we'll have to remove you."

"We're not going anywhere; heaven is for weaklings who can't defend themselves."

"Your wife Joan is in heaven, and she's been waiting for you for a long time. She says you're very stubborn, but eventually, you realise that you're not always right."

"How do you know about Joan? Is she here?"

"No, but she knows you are; I've been talking to her while we've been discussing things."

"Can I see her?"

"Yes, but you would have to go to heaven. Do you want to?"

"From what I've seen I can't see us staying here, and it would be wonderful to see her again."

"OK, let's get all those who want to go together and then I want you all to open your eyes and tell me what you can see."

"We can all see a bright light; it wasn't there before, though."

"No, because you weren't looking in the right way. That's the entrance to heaven, and we're going to go into that light."

"It's getting closer, and I can see vague shapes of people."

"Yes, you will be able to see them better as we get closer. Do you recognise any of them?"

"Yes, they are my parents, and here comes Joan. I'm going now if that's alright."

"Yes, go in peace."

As Danny opened his eyes, he smiled. "Bit of a turnaround wasn't it; one minute he was going nowhere, and then he can't wait to go."

"Yes, it's amazing how they change when they know their family is waiting."

"Is that all of them?" Caroline asked.

"Yes, but I would like Danny to give you and Sheila some healing just to settle you down if that's alright."

"Yes, that would be OK. How does that work?"

"Danny will stand behind you and place his hands on your shoulders, and his guides will give you healing to balance you out a bit. It's also a way of making sure we haven't missed anyone who has attached themselves to you."

"OK, shall I go first?"

"Yes, that's fine. You only have to relax and sit quietly."

While Danny was giving healing, I walked around the house just checking each room to make sure everything was calm, which it was.

When I came back, Sheila was just finishing her healing, and I said, "If you wish to develop your mediumship or see if you have the ability, why don't you contact the spiritualist church in Gosport? I believe they have an awareness circle on Mondays where everyone is welcome. You can find out if you're mediumistic and the best way to go forward for you. I would advise you to leave it for a few weeks while you settle down from this though before you go."

"I think I'll wait for myself to calm down before I go there and try to sort my life out then maybe. I just want to be normal right now."

"That's the right way to look at it; you can always consider your options at another time. If you've got it, it won't go away," I said. "Now that your house has been cleared you should have better nights. The protection that's been placed around your house will stop any others coming to bother you unless you go looking for them. We can't stop you if you want to contact the spirit world, but after what you've been through maybe, you can do it the right way, in a controlled environment at the church."

"We won't do anything like that again; we're just glad there are people like you who can help," Caroline said.

"It's a pleasure to help; now we'll leave you in peace," Danny said.

It's interesting to note although the previous cases started in different ways, the people always thought it was spirits of dead people and not demons or the devil. I wonder if this is because they were not so religious and had not been indoctrinated into the beliefs of religion.

A Haunting in Atlanta USA

I was contacted through my website and asked if I could help someone in Atlanta who was having major problems. I asked what the problems were and was told things were being moved and some of the rooms were freezing even in the hot weather. There were noises and whispering and the lady Janice was very moody. Her emotions were all over the place and although Janice had seen the doctor they had just put her on medication to calm her down, they weren't stopping the interference. Although she wasn't so moody when she took the drug, it didn't stop things moving, and Janice still heard the noises and whispering, so she knew it wasn't her. She had some paranormal investigators check the place out, and they said there were spirits there and sprinkled holy water and burned sage but to no effect. Could we help her to get rid of the discarnate spirits that were on the verge of driving her out of their house?

I asked if the paranormal investigators had ascertained why the spirits were there. Janice said they told her it was a man who had died in the house and he didn't want them living in his house.

I said we would do a remote clearance for them and asked how long it had been going on. Janice said it started just after she moved in with noises and then things got moved, and she started getting headaches and gradually things got worse. It had been going on for six months, and they didn't know where to turn for help. They had been to the church, and they had come and said prayers and again sprinkled holy water. Janice said it went quiet for a few days and then came back stronger. Was there anything we could do?

I asked her to describe the layout of the house and herself so we could tune into the right home and when we next had our circle we would see what we could do.

On the next circle night, I asked the sitters to tune in and tell me the layout and description of the house and the occupants. The reason for this was to make sure they were tuning into the right house. After a few false starts, one of our group described the house and some of the décor, and another sitter tuned into that information and described Janice.

Once I was happy that we were all working on the same property, I asked them to tell me about the spirits in the house. Danny described a man of about forty, five foot six and quite thin, with a smug smile, black hair, and dirty fingernails. He was unshaven and had cold looking eyes… not a very nice man from the feelings he was picking up. We all tuned into him and I asked Danny to bring him through. The following is what transpired:

"Good evening," I said.

"Where am I and what do you want?"

"We've brought you here so we can have a chat about what you've been doing in our friend's house."

"That's none of your business."

"Well, actually it is as our friend has given us permission to deal with the likes of you on her behalf. Let's start with your name."

"Why do you want to know my name?"

"We can talk to each other in a less formal way. My name's Mike; what's yours?"

"Jeremy if you must know. Now, why don't you go away and leave me alone?"

"We can't do that; you don't belong in our friend's house, and we're here to either help you or remove you from the home. What've you been doing there?"

"I just do what I like; what's it to you?"

"You're upsetting the people who live there, and it's got to stop; you weren't invited, and you're not wanted there."

"Who's going to stop me? Just because you've brought me here doesn't mean you can stop me going back, you can't keep me here forever."

"We don't have to; we've put protection around the house so even if you try you won't get back in. We would like to help you if you let us. Do you want to carry on annoying people?"

"What else is there to do?"

"Well, you could go to heaven and be with your family."

"Why should I believe you? They had other people go there; they were trying to banish me to hell. They burnt some grass or something, all it did was make the place smell. I just went upstairs until they'd gone. They threw water around as well, don't know why. Then they had some priest come and say prayers; he read out of the bible and tried to send me away, but I just ignored him. I'm not religious, and all that mumbo jumbo is a lot of nonsense. If they couldn't send me to hell, what makes you think you can take me to heaven, if there is one?"

"There is a heaven. We know that because we've taken many people there; they have met their families and some of them were like you, they didn't believe there was such a place. Where do you think you came from when you were born? What do you think you are now you're not physical anymore? Your body has died, yet you're still here talking to me? How do you think we brought you from America where you were, to here in England?"

"I don't know; perhaps it's a trick, although you're right about one thing, if I'm dead, how am I talking to you. OK, let's see what else you can do."

"Alright, open your eyes and tell me what you can see."

"My eyes are open, and all I can see is this place and the dark outside. I can see a few others around, but they aren't very nice."

"You mean they're like you?"

"No, they're nasty; what am I supposed to be looking for?"

"You'll know when you see it; humour me and make an effort to open your eyes, then you'll see what I'm talking about."

"Oh, I can see a big light; it's like it's at the end of a tunnel."

"That's where your family is, would you like to see them?"

"Show me then."

"OK, I won't take you to heaven yet as you're not ready, but I will show you what Kathleen looks like and your son Ed, who are waiting for you."

"How do you know about them? Are you reading my mind?"

"No, when I tune into you, my guides connect me to your family who are in heaven. Here they are."

"I don't know what guides are, but they're clever... that's my wife and son. My son was only 30 when I died; how come he's dead?"

"He died in his seventies from a stroke. You've been dead a long time. Do you want to be with them?"

"If you're sure they'll let me in. I haven't been very kind to those people whose house I've been in."

"We know, but now's the time to change all that, and being with your family will help. Are you ready?"

"I'm as ready as I'll ever be."

"OK, here we go. There, what can you see now?"

"There are lots of people that I've seen before I died. My wife and all my children are here; how is that possible, they were all too young to die?"

"What year did you die?"

"It was 1956, I think."

"Well, it is 2012, so you've been dead 56 years now, so it's entirely possible, isn't it?"

"Really, I've been dead that long, it just seems like yesterday. When I think about it there doesn't appear to be any time here."

"It is a long time, but not so long as some; would you like to join them?"

"Yes please. I'm sorry for causing any upsets, please forgive me."

"The fact that you're going to heaven means you're not a bad man, just misled. Go in peace."

He went across and we watched him being greeted by his family, one less to cause trouble for the living now he was safely back home. Danny came out of trance and said, "He was overwhelmed by it all, but I could feel his gratitude at finding his family again."

I asked the others if they were aware of anyone else at the house and Mary said, "There's a lady dressed in a dark green dress with curly grey hair; she's about 65 and five foot two inches tall, a bit cuddly. Looks like a typical grandmother, but she's not as nice as she appears."

"She's got a lot of children with her, and there are two other ladies there as well," I said.

"Yes that's right; shall I bring the women through?" Mary asked.

"Yes OK, let's see what she has to say."

Mary went into a light trance and brought the old lady through.

"Hello," I said. "How can we help you?"

"Who are you and what do you want, and where am I?"

"My name is Mike, and we want to talk to you, and you're in my house."

"Well first, I don't speak to strangers, and second, I want to be taken back to where I was, we have made that place safe for the children. I must get back to make sure they're safe."

"The children are safe, and maybe after we have spoken, they will be able to go to where they belong."

"Well hurry up, what do you want?"

"I want to know why you've collected so many children and what you're going to do with them."

"We pick up lost children and bring them back to the house. We tell them they're dead and we're going to look after them and give them a job, to keep them out of mischief."

"What sort of job?"

"Whatever I decide needs doing."

"Like what for instance?"

"Sometimes we have to tidy up; things have to be in their right place you know."

"So you show the children how to move things."

"Yes, how else can they do their job if we don't show them how?"

"But the things you move aren't yours. You can upset people by keeping moving things so they can't find them."

"That's alright, they should be tidier, and then we wouldn't have to pick up behind them."

"What else do the children have to do?"

"Nothing except getting better; some of them have pains that they are always complaining about. When they get too close to the people in the house, they feel the pain and think it's theirs. We try to tell the children they're alright and they don't have any pain, but it's difficult."

"I see, so why don't you take their pain away then they wouldn't pass it on to the people living there?"

"We've tried, but it doesn't work."

"OK, would you like to go to heaven? We could take the children and your friends. You'll be safe then and not have any pain?"

"If we could find heaven we would have gone a long time ago. Do you know where it is?"

"Yes, we can take you there. Let's get everyone together and take their pain away. Now, can you open your eyes and tell me what you see?"

"I can see a light; it's very bright. Did you take everyone's pain away?"

"No, our friends did. That light is the entrance to heaven; if everyone is ready, we'll take you there."

"Yes, we're all ready."

"OK off we go, it won't take long; what can you see now?"

"I can see all the children going to different groups of people, and they're smiling so I know they aren't hurting anymore. Oh, there's my mother and father, and my husband. I had better get off now, thank you for your help from all of us, goodbye."

"Goodbye."

Mary came out of trance and she was a bit emotional when she saw all those children going home. "That was a bit heavy," she said. "All those poor children who were lost, there were a lot of tears of happiness from everybody... it certainly gets to you."

Once Mary had settled down we checked the house out and found a nasty looking man hiding from us; he felt horrible. I asked Danny to bring him through as I was aware he didn't like women and would have been harder to deal with if Mary had brought him through.

When he came through he was furious.

"What the hell do you think you're doing interfering with my house?"

"We were asked to remove the spirits from the house so the people could get some peace, and maybe straighten out their lives, without your interference, so that's what we're doing."

"You've no right to mess about with my house, leave us alone."

"It's OK for you to say that but you left us no choice when you started to upset people's lives. I'm afraid you and your friends have to leave."

"You can't do anything to stop us so go away."

"What have you been doing there?"

"That's my business now go away; I'm not going to talk to you anymore."

"That's a pity because by talking we might be able to resolve the problems for everyone. You know we can't let you go back, but we can help you to improve your situation."

"How, are you going to give me another house to work in?"

"Don't be silly, we're going to make your life easier so you'll have some time for yourself, instead of chasing about making sure no one gets away."

"How are you going to do that?"

"We're going to take all the people you've captured and take them to heaven, and then we're going to offer to take your helpers and you, if you want, to heaven as well."

"I'm not going to let you talk to them so you can't."

I asked Danny to put protection around him so he couldn't interfere but to allow him to watch. I then asked Mary to bring through a lady who was working with him.

When Mary brought the woman through she seemed a little subdued, considering what she had been doing.

"Hello, what's your name?" I asked.

"Julie, sir, what's going to happen to me?"

"Well, Julie, what have you been doing?"

"I only did what I was told to do. I was making people argue and feel unhappy; it wasn't just me, there are a lot of us if we didn't do it he would do it to us."

"Well, he can only watch now; do you all want to get away from him?"

"Yes, we've tried, but he just sends some nasty men to bring us back."

"He won't be able to do that now; as you can see, he can't move, and you're protected by that blue light around you. Would you like to go to heaven?"

"Yes please, can you take all of us?"

"We can take everyone who wants to go. Now, open your eyes and tell me what you can see."

"I can see a light. It's at the end of a long tunnel, what is it?"

"That's the entrance to heaven. If everyone's ready, we'll take you there OK?"

"Yes, we're ready; he can't come after us can he?"

"No, let's go, it won't take long. Now, what can you see?"

"There's my mum and dad and my grandparents... are you sure he can't catch me again?"

"Yes, I'm sure, go in peace."

When Mary came back, I asked Danny to bring the man back.

"Why are you doing this? It's not fair. I've spent a long time getting the right people in my house, and now you've taken them away?"

"We've taken them to heaven where they can be at peace with their loved ones… would you like to join them? There's nothing left here for you now unless you want to start all over again somewhere else?"

"I am not going to heaven or anywhere else, I'm staying here."

"Sorry, can't let you stay. The people in the house want you gone, and if you don't want to go to heaven, we'll have to send you back out into the cold and dark."

"Do your worst, I'll be back in no time."

"You noticed the protection we put around you so you couldn't interfere just now; well, that will stay with you and you will not be able to get back into the house. Also, you'll be unable to interfere with anyone else for a long time; now, you're free to go."

Our guides collected him and took him away where he would be looked after and helped to see the error of his ways.

We checked the house out again with our senses, and all were quite happy that there were no spirits left to cause any problems.

The following day I e-mailed Janice and asked how things were. She said they'd had a good night and the atmosphere was lighter and a lot more relaxed. I said I would contact her in a couple of weeks, which I did, and she told me it was like living in a different house. Janice said she was feeling much better in herself and she wasn't losing things anymore. I explained about the protection that our guides had put round her house and assured her she would have no more problems, providing she didn't look for spirits. She said she wasn't even going to think about it, and while she didn't know what I had done, she thanked me from the bottom of her heart. We said goodbye – another successful outcome I'm happy to say. As you can see, distance is not a problem; we just get our guides to bring them to us.

You may be wondering, if our guides can remove the spirits from the house, then why don't they do it all the time and why do they need us. Yes, they can remove them, but that would be going against the free will of both the spirits and the people in the house. We don't know what the people or the spirits' lessons are, and by removing them without explaining what's going on, we may be interfering with their education. Also, by us working on this side of life, we can connect with the discarnate spirit easier as their awareness is still on the physical. More often than not they are unaware of the spirit world until we show them. What takes us a couple of hours can take our guides months, as they first have to be noticed before they can talk to the spirits who are lost. Yes, they can influence the spirit's minds, but it's a long drawn-out business when we can get through to them in a matter of hours.

A Haunting in Chichester, West Sussex

We got a call from a local church asking if we could help a lady called Sarah, whose three-year-old son was frightened to go into his bedroom. It seemed he had a man in his bedroom who was saying to him: "Get out! This is my room! Don't come in here anymore."

I telephoned Sarah and asked her what was going on. Sarah told me how her little boy who was frightened to go in his bedroom at night, would play quite happily with his two-year-old sister during the day. It was only a few weeks ago, that he had started crying when he went to bed. Sarah said the only way she could get him to sleep was to put him in her bed and lie down with him. His sister who shared the same bedroom as him was quite happy and went to sleep with no problems. I asked if Sarah knew why he was frightened, and she said he had seen a man in his room who kept telling him to get out. She said after tea he would start getting agitated and he got worse as he got nearer to going to bed. Now he was sleeping in her room every night, and because he didn't have to go to his bed, he was feeling better. Sarah asked if we could do anything to help. I said I thought so, and arranged to go and see her along with Danny.

When we arrived, Sarah, who was in her early twenties, showed us the bedroom and told us she couldn't understand why her daughter wasn't aware of the man in the room. We talked to her little boy who said that he could see an old man sitting in the corner of his room; the man was there only at night. Because of the little boy's age, we didn't want to frighten him, so we told him we would put the man in prison and he wouldn't see him anymore. While checking the room, we became aware of two other men and three women, so we collected them all up to deal with once we'd left the flat. The little boy was playing with his sister and it was hard to talk to him because being so young he was busy playing. They were watching a children's programme on the television. I wanted to check him out, so I asked Sarah if I could pick him up to show him what was on the TV, which she said was OK. I picked him up, and while doing so, I was aware of two men and three women around him, and also two children who were attached to him. I took them off him so we could talk to them after we had left. Reassuring the mother that everything was cleared, Danny and I returned to my car where Danny went into a light trance and brought them through one at a time.

We told the little boy that everything would be alright now, as the man would never come back once he was in prison. As he wasn't aware of the others, we didn't say anything.

The first person we brought through was the man who was frightening the little boy; the man is in his sixties, and I suppose to a little boy, he would look frightening in the dark. The man didn't know that he had died, so I asked him his name, which he said was Stuart.

"Hello, Stuart, what's troubling you?"

"I don't know where I am, and don't know what's happened to me. I have pain in my chest, and my head hurts... can you help, please?

"Yes, we will try. Can you tell me, what's the last thing you remember before you found yourself where you are now?"

"I was coming down the stairs when I felt a pain in my chest; everything went dark, that's all I remember, and then I was here."

"Do you think you may have had a heart attack?" I asked.

"Is that what happened to me, have I died?"

"Yes, I'm afraid it is; it seems that you fell when you had your heart attack, which is why your head hurts. What do you think happens to people when they die?" I asked.

"I don't know; when you're dead you're dead, which is strange because I could see a little boy and his sister playing in the room I was in. The little boy was quite noisy, which hurt my head, so I told him not to come in the room."

"Did you know he could see you and because nobody else could he was frightened of you; to him, you were a strange man who he didn't know."

"I'm sorry I didn't mean to scare him, and I didn't think, I was confused, I couldn't work out where I was or what had happened to me. So, you tell me I died; obviously, there is something more, but I can't believe this is it."

"You are quite right there is a place called heaven, and no doubt you've heard people talk about it. That's where people go when they die."

"Where is this place you call heaven? And if it's what I've heard it is, then I would like to go there because I understand if it's true, my family are there."

"It's where everybody goes when they die; your parents, your loved ones and your friends, will all go there eventually. Sometimes like yourself, people get lost, but over a period of time, most people find their way to heaven. The reason you haven't is that you thought there was nothing more once you had died; fortunately, we're able to take you there if you would like."

"Yes please; how do I get there?"

"If you would open your eyes and tell me what you can see."

"It's brighter over there; it's like there's a light in the distance. I haven't seen that before."

"That light is coming from heaven. Would you like me to take you there? I'm sure you'll find your family waiting for you."

"Yes please. I'm sorry about the little boy. I hope he'll be alright."

"He'll be fine; shall we go into the light?"

"It's getting a lot closer, and it's quite warm. Will my wife by there?"

"What year did you die?"

"It was 1974. I haven't been here very long."

"It's 2015, so it's 41 years since you died."

"Good Lord, it doesn't seem that long. I can see people now. I see my mother, and now I can see my wife. I would like to go now if that's alright."

"Yes, go in peace."

Danny watched him go and then opened his eyes. "Poor old soul; still, he'll be OK now."

"Yes, he wasn't nasty, just confused. Shall we have a word with one of the ladies now?"

"Yes OK, which one do you want me to bring through?"

"The oldest one; the one wearing a cardigan over a blue dress."

I waited a moment while Danny brought her through then asked: "Am I talking to Mavis?"

"Yes, dear, and what's your name?"

"I'm called Mike, how are you?"

"I'm all right, thank you. That poor man was very confused; will he be alright now?"

"Yes, he'll be fine; now, what about you and your friends, can we take you home as well?"

"Yes please, we've been here a while."

"Why are you here?"

"We've been to lots of places and arrived here a little while ago; we can't seem to find this place you call heaven. There are a lot of unhappy people here that we've come across, confused, frightened and lonely."

"You don't seem afraid?"

"No, we have our faith, we know we'll find heaven when the time is right. We've been trying to help the poor souls, but unfortunately, we couldn't take them to heaven as we don't know the way."

"We can help you there, if you and your friends or should I say sisters, would open your eyes, I'm sure you'll see the entrance to heaven."

"That would have to be that big light; we knew God would send a messenger to find us and bring us home. Would it be alright to go now?"

"Yes, if you'd like to come with me, I will take you there."

"Thank you, that's very kind."

We took them to heaven where they met other sisters from their convent, and we said goodbye.

Danny opened his eyes when he knew they were safe. I asked him to bring through the young boy who was waiting to talk to us.

"Hello," I said when he came through. "Do you know what's happened to you?"

"Hello yes, I'm dead, it's a funny feeling knowing that you're dead and still be able to walk around and talk to people. I used to play with that little girl in that house we were in; she wasn't frightened of me. Where did those nuns go?"

"They went to heaven to be with their friends and family; would you and your friend like to go also?"

"Can you take us there?"

"Yes, that's why we're here, to help you find your way home to your family. If you and your friend would like to open your eyes, what do you see now?"

"I can see a brilliant light and people who I couldn't see before. Is that light where heaven is?"

"Yes, we're going to go into the light where your family is, and you will be safe then."

"My friend has a lot of pain all over her body; will that go away?"

"We'll take it away as we go to heaven; she'll no longer be in pain by the time we get there."

"Thank you, I can see my mummy and daddy. Can I go now?"

"Yes, you'll be alright now, so will your friend. Bye."

"Bye, and thank you, mister."

Danny opened his eyes and said, "I'm not aware of anyone else, are you?"

"No, it's all clear now, and the little boy in the flat will be OK now. I'll give her a call in about a week to make sure everything's OK."

A week later I gave Sarah a call and asked how her little boy was. She said he was fine and he was sleeping in his bed without any problems. "He says the man is not there anymore because those two men that came to our house, took him away."

It's interesting to see that a little boy of three years old who had no idea about God, devils, angels or spirits, still had problems. He had no belief at this stage in anything, other than being a little boy. So what he thought was a nasty old man was in fact just the man who was lost. Older people may have seen the old man but may also have seen something else i.e. a ghost in whatever form they expected to see them or any of the different "demons" that people believe in. Even if the old man had been a negative spirit that little boy would have seen the old man, yet an adult could well have seen something different according to their beliefs and expectations.

Conclusion

I have looked at how religions started with belief in ancestor worship and how the primitive ideas of early man made up gods of all sorts to help them in their daily lives. How religion changed and the belief in one God affected the thinking and views of humankind. I have also looked at the philosophies of some of the major religions and how they embraced the idea of the Devil and demons. How superstition has played a big part in forming the ideas and beliefs of modern society. How what you believe can be manifest to create fear of what is nothing more than a person who has died and can influence or interact with the living from beyond the grave. The lengths some religions will go to keep control of the population at least in the early to Middle Ages. How fear has driven humankind to believe in a saviour who will rescue them from devils and demons regardless of their actions. The belief in religious rituals to overcome the evil from the spirit world that is in fact only people who have died and either got lost or wish to control the living from their side of life.

I have discussed the reasons why spirits get lost and how and why they affect the living in the way they do. How not everything that happens that is unexplained initially, is spirit interference, but may require further investigation before a diagnosis is considered. Disease and mental illness were first thought to be the work of the Devil, yet with medical advances it can be seen to be a physical problem not spiritual. The fact there is a thin line between some mental illness and spirit interference, and that we should be very careful not to condemn people to life on medication without first investigating all possibilities.

I have looked at some well-known cases of exorcisms done by religious institutions, and it's clear the individuals are very religious and accept the doctrines of their religion to their detriment.

I have presented some case histories to show that the interfering spirits are intelligent, and reason will very often resolve the problems they are causing. By explaining the situation to the discarnate spirit and the person being haunted, things can be resolved without dramatics. If the person being haunted has strong beliefs or fears of spirit interference, they sometimes have trouble believing the interfering spirits have gone. They will try to see if they can still detect discarnate spirits around them and of course, they will. That is because they are opening up to what may be, and inadvertently tuning in. By staying tuned in and not focusing on the physical, they will draw other spirits to them and will continue to experience interference. Sometimes if you look for something you may just find it whether you want it or not. To the spirit, it is an invitation to come and interact not necessarily in a nice way. That is why we tell people to forget about spirit and get on with their lives. Mediums have trained to recognise and control what they are aware of, most people are not and are unable to close their mind to the spirit world.

Further Reading

Celtic Mythology [online en.wikipedia.org/wiki. Celtic. mythology]

Religions of the Ancient Near East. [anthropology.ua.edu/blogs]

Magic in the ancient world [online Wikipedia]

Necromancy [online Wikipedia]

Witchcraft [online Wikipedia]

Spirit possession [online Wikipedia]

William J. Baldwin, Ph.D. Healing Lost Souls ISBN 1-57174-366-9

Bibliography

An Intellectual look at death and the afterlife (April 1991) [Accessed 9/11/15] www.soc.hawaii.edu/leon.

A Natural history of gargoyles. The blue dot.com [Accessed 5/11/15]

Gargoyles [Accessed 5/11/15] Wikipedia.

Ghosts in Tibetan Culture [Accessed 4/11/15] Wikipedia.

Hinduism [Accessed 4/11/15] Wikipedia.

Witch Hunt [Accessed 29/11/15] Wikipedia.

Necromancy [Accessed 22/10/15] Wikipedia.

Exorcism [Accessed 22/10/15] Wikipedia.

Zoroastrianism [Accessed 22/10/15] Wikipedia.

Religion in the Middle Ages [Accessed 22/10/15] www.thefinertimes.com

Middle Ages more about religion [Accessed 22/10/15] www.learners.org

Superstition during the Dark Ages [Accessed 22/10/15] www.answers.com

45606103R00150

Printed in Poland
by Amazon Fulfillment
Poland Sp. z o.o., Wrocław